The Cambridge English Course

2
Student's Book

Michael Swan and Catherine Walter

Cambridge University Press

Cambridge   London   New York   New Rochelle   Melbourne   Sydney

ISBN 0 521 28984 X   Student's Book 2

Split edition: ISBN 0 521 33757 7   Part A
ISBN 0 521 33758 5   Part B
ISBN 0 521 33759 3   Part C

ISBN 0 521 28983 1   Practice Book 2
ISBN 0 521 31626 X   Test Book 2
ISBN 0 521 28982 3   Teacher's Book 2
ISBN 0 521 24817 5   Cassette Set 2
ISBN 0 521 30324 9   Student's Cassette 2

...ed
...ously
...

...e Press Syndicate of the University of Cambridge
...ding, Trumpington Street, Cambridge CB2 1RP
...7th Street, New York, NY 10022, USA
...amford Road, Oakleigh, Melbourne 3166, Australia

© Cambridge University Press 1985

First published 1985
Fourth printing 1986

Designed by John Youé and Associates, Croydon, Surrey
Typeset by Text Filmsetters Limited, London
Origination by BTA Reprographics Limited, London
Printed in Great Britain by Blantyre Printing and Binding, Glasgow

Authors' acknowledgements

We are grateful to all the people who have helped us with this book. Our thanks to:

The many people whose ideas have influenced our work, including all the colleagues and students from whom we have learnt.

Ruth Gairns, Stuart Redman, Alan Duff, Alan Maley, Mario Rinvolucri and Penny Ur, for specific ideas and exercises we have borrowed.

Those institutions and teachers who were kind enough to work with the Pilot Edition of this course, and whose comments have done so much to shape the final version.

Peter Roach for his expert and sensible help with the phonetic transcription.

John Youé, Jack Wood, Margaret Dodd, Tanya Ball, Alison Pincott, Jane Molineaux, Jason Youé and Helen Lawrence of John Youé and Associates, for their invaluable help in the design and production of the book.

John and Angela Eckersley, and the staff of the Eckersley School of English, Oxford, for making it possible for us to try out the Pilot Edition of the course in their classrooms.

Ken Blissett, John and Rita Peake, Alexandra Phillips, Pat Robbins, Sue Ward, Adrian Webber, Jane and Keith Woods, for agreeing to be questioned within earshot of our microphones.

Mark, for all his help and support.

And finally, to Adrian du Plessis, Peter Donovan, Jeanne McCarten and Peter Ducker of Cambridge University Press, for their creativity, their understanding, and their outstanding professional competence.

Michael Swan   *Catherine Walter*

The authors and publishers would like to thank the following people and institutions for their help in testing the material and for the invaluable feedback which they provided:

The British Council, Thessaloniki, Greece; The British School, Florence, Italy; Australian College of English, Sydney, Australia; University of Berne, Berne, Switzerland; Études Pédagogiques de l'Enseignement Secondaire, Geneva, Switzerland; The Bell School, Cambridge; Bell College, Saffron Waldon; Oxford Language Centre, Oxford; The British Institute, Rome, Italy; The Newnham Language Centre, Cambridge; Adult Migrant Education Services, Melbourne, Australia; Communication in Business, Paris, France; Studio School of English, Cambridge; International House, Arezzo, Italy; Grange School, Santiago, Chile; Eurocentre, Cambridge; Gillian Porter-Ladousse, Paris, France; Pauline Bramall, Karlsruhe, W. Germany; College de Saussure, Geneva, Switzerland; Noreen O'Shea, Paris, France, Eurocentre, Brighton, New School of English, Cambridge; Eckersley School, Oxford; Central School of English, London; Anglo-Continental School, Bournemouth; Godmer House School of English, Oxford; School of English Studies, Folkestone; Davies's School of English, London; Oxford Language Centre, Oxford; Regent School, Rome, Italy; Brunswick Education Centre, Victoria, Australia.

Contents

Map of Book 2*

In Unit	FUNCTIONS AND SKILLS Students will learn to	NOTIONS, TOPICS AND SITUATIONS Students will learn to talk about
1	Make introductions; ask for and give information; describe people; listen for specific information.	Themselves and their interests, people's appearance and behaviour.
2	Make commentaries; express doubt and certainty; take part in simple discussions.	Appearance of things; beliefs.
3	Narrate; express past time relations.	Accidents; basic office situations.
4	Describe; compare.	Similarities and differences; people's appearance.
5	Ask for things without knowing the exact word; make and reply to suggestions, requests and offers.	Shopping; household goods; clothes.
6	Predict; speak on the phone; negotiate.	Probability; certainty; the future; appointments.
7	Ask for and give information.	People's experiences and habits; national and local news; duration; changes.
8	Improve scan reading skills; link written texts; explain reasons for a choice; make reverse-charge phone calls.	Travelling to and in Britain and the US; holidays.
9	Ask for and give information; narrate; apologise and accept apologies; make excuses; link written texts.	Emergencies; causation; blame and responsibility.
10	Predict; deduce; describe processes; give instructions.	Conditions and probability; superstitions; cooking.
REVISION 11	Use what they have learnt in different ways.	Employment; they will revise vocabulary.
12	Ask for explanations; describe processes; express doubt and certainty.	Manufacturing and other processes; causes of past events.
13	Ask for and give directions; describe; define.	Landscapes; towns; houses; objects.
14	Ask about and express preferences; connect written text; express agreement and disagreement.	Relatives; family life.
15	Express wants, hopes and intentions; ask for favours; agree to requests; thank and reply to thanks.	Jobs; leisure activities.
16	Express opinions; negotiate.	Personal expenditure; budgets; quantity.
17	Narrate; ask for and give information; link written texts.	Time relations; habits.
18	Express opinions; report; use dictionaries when reading.	History; scientific discoveries; probability.
19	Make small talk: greet; welcome; ask for and give opinions; ask for repetition; take leave.	Job routines; food; entertainment.
20	Give instructions; give opinions; suggest; persuade; warn.	Housework; plans; the notion of orientation; personal problems.
21	Express preferences, opinion and obligation; complain.	Electrical appliances; breakdowns in common possessions.
REVISION 22	Use what they have learnt in different ways.	No new topics.
23	Give information; express positive and negative emotions; ask for and give advice.	Emotions; moods; personal relationships.
24	Express degrees of formality; ask for and give permission.	Authority; government; plans.
25	Ask for and give information; express likes and dislikes; negotiate; suggest.	Art and music.
26	Express notions of classification and deduction; paraphrase.	Animals and man; household objects.
27	Express possibilities; ask for and give information; hypothesize; describe.	Changes in people and things.
28	Express opinions and hypotheses; complain; ask for and give details.	Illness and health.
29	Express wishes; report states of knowledge.	Intelligence and memory.
30	Ask for and express opinions; ask for and give information.	Work; job routines.
31	Enquire formally; give directions; explain; request.	Means of transport; travel by car.
REVISION 32	Use what they have learnt in different ways.	No new topics.

*This 'map' of the course should be translated into students' language where possible.

VOCABULARY: Students will learn about 1,000 common words and expressions during the course.

GRAMMAR	PHONOLOGY
Students will learn or revise these grammar points	**Students will study these aspects of pronunciation**
Simple present; *be* and *have*; *have got*; adverbs of degree; *like . . . ing*, no article for general meaning.	Hearing unstressed syllables in rapid speech.
Present progressive; contrast between simple present and present progressive.	/ɪ/ and /iː/; pronunciations of *th*.
Regular and irregular past tenses; past progressive; *when-* and *while*-clauses; ellipsis.	Hearing final consonants; pronunciations of the letter *a*.
Comparative and superlative of adjectives; *than* and *as*; relative clauses with *who*; *do* as pro-verb; compound adjectives.	Decoding rapid speech; stress, rhythm and linking.
At a + shop; *a thing with a . . .* ; *a thing for . . . ing*; modal verbs; infinitive with and without *to*.	Rhythm and stress; /eɪ/ versus /e/; spellings of /eɪ/.
May; *will*; *going to*; present progressive as future; prepositions of time.	/əʊ/; 'dark' *l*; stress and rhythm.
Present perfect simple; present perfect progressive; non-progressive verbs; *since*; *for*; *used to*.	Letter *e* stressed and unstressed at the beginning of words.
Can for possibility; *may* and *will*; linking devices for writing.	/ʃ/ and /tʃ/; rising and falling intonation.
Present perfect and its contrast with simple past; *there has been*; *make* + object + adjective or infinitive; past progressive.	/θ/ and /ð/; decoding conversational expressions spoken at speed.
If-clauses in open conditions; *if* vs *when*; imperatives; present tense as future in subordinate clauses; *when* and *until*.	/ɪ/; pronunciations of the letter *a*.
General revision.	Fluency practice.
Simple present passive; past passive; present and past participles; question forms.	Hearing /ə/; /h/; decoding rapid speech.
Imperatives; *there is/are*; *feel/smell* + adjective; relative pronouns and their omission; preposition at end of clause.	Decoding rapid speech; /iː/, /ɪ/ and /aɪ/; pronunciations of the letter *i*.
Would rather; *should*.	Linking with /r/, /j/, and /w/; sentence stress.
Want, *would like*, and *would love*; *want* + object + infinitive; *hope/going/try to*; *I/We wondered if* + past.	/əʊ/; decoding rapid speech.
Must and *can*; quantifiers; *will* for proposals; *too/enough to . . .*	Linking, liaison and assimilation.
Time clauses with *as soon as*, *before*, *after*, *until*; *still*, *yet*, *already*; *such* and *so*; past perfect.	/ɒ/, /ɔː/, /əʊ/ and their spellings; decoding rapid speech.
Reported speech; *used to*; word order in reported questions; modals; *likely*; *say* and *tell*.	Rhythm; initial consonant clusters beginning with *s*.
Question-tags; prepositions in questions; *so/neither (do I)*.	Intonation of question tags; fluency practice.
Infinitive of purpose; *by . . . ing*; *had better*; negative imperatives; hypothetical conditions; *ought to*; *Let's*; *Why don't*.	Consonant clusters with *ex*, final consonant clusters.
Should; phrasal verbs; present tenses; simple past; *won't* = refuses to.	Spellings of final /ə/; decoding fast speech.
General revision.	Exceptions to general rules about spelling/pronunciation links; fluency practice.
Let + object + infinitive; questions with *who* as subject and object.	/ə/; initial consonant clusters.
Simple present active and passive; *who* and *which* relative clauses; *must*, *have to*, *will have to*; emphatic imperatives.	Strong and weak forms of *must*.
Quantifiers; word formation; passives, and passive questions with final prepositions; interrogative *which* and *what*.	Pronunciations of *r*; intonation.
Although; relative clauses; articles; *a . . . one*.	Stress for emphasis, weak and strong forms.
Get-structures; past conditional.	Unstressed initial /ə/ and /ɪ/.
Verbs with two objects; relative *who* and *that*; frequency adverbs; reported commands.	Linking.
Wish + past tense.	Word stress.
Adverbs of manner with past participles; *have to*.	Pronunciations of the letter *u*; pronunciations of *au* and *ou*.
Deixis (*come/go*, *here/there*, *this/that*); modals of obligation.	/ə/ in unstressed syllables; /θ/ and /ð/.
General revision.	Fluency practice.

People

A Tell me about yourself

1 Listen to the conversations and practise the sentences.
Introduce yourself to some other students. Find out their names and where they come from.
Then introduce some students to each other.

WHEREABOUTS IN INDIA?

RECEPTION

5th International TBU C

2 Match the questions and the answers.

1. What nationality are you?
2. Do you do any sport?
3. What kind of music do you like?
4. What kind of books do you read?
5. Are you shy?
6. Can you play the piano?
7. What do you like doing in your spare time?
8. Why are you learning English?
9. Where do you live?
10. Do you like watching football matches?
11. What does your father look like?
12. What's your mother like?
13. Have you got any brothers or sisters?
14. How do you feel about snakes?

a. Knitting and reading.
b. Mostly novels; sometimes history books.
c. Austrian.
d. She's very calm and cheerful.
e. In a small town near Vienna.
f. No, I'm fairly self-confident.
g. They don't interest me.
h. I prefer playing games to watching them.
i. Classical music.
j. He's tall and fair.
k. Yes, long-distance running.
l. I'd like to travel more, and I think it's a useful language.
m. Yes, two sisters.
n. Yes, but not very well.

3 Here are some answers. What are the questions?

1. Carlos Peña.
2. Venezuela.
3. I'm an engineer.
4. Twenty-five.
5. One metre seventy-eight.
6. Two brothers and a sister.
7. No, I'm not.
8. In a small flat in Caracas.
9. I need to read it for my work.
10. No, but I can speak a little French.
11. I watch TV or I go out with friends.
12. No, I don't, but I like dancing.
13. About twice a week.

4 Write some more questions to ask people in the class. You can ask the teacher for help, like this:

'How do you say marié?' 'Married.'
'What's the English for Leichtathletik?' 'Athletics.'
'How do you pronounce "archaeology"?'
'How do you spell ....?'
'What does "hobby" mean?'
'Is this correct: "............"?'

5 Interview the teacher. Find out as much as possible about him/her.

6 Work in pairs. Interview your partner and find out as much as possible about him/her.

7 Work in groups of four. Tell the other two students about your partner from Exercise 6.

8 Study the Summary on page 134.

7

B Married with two children

1 Copy the table. Then listen to the descriptions of the five people and fill in the details. Here are some of the words and expressions you will hear.

JOBS: nurse; secretary; policewoman; printer's reader; works with racehorses; part-time.

BUILD: slim; heavily built.

CLOTHES: shirt; blouse; sweater; T-shirt; trousers; jeans; skirt; ear-ring; olive green; striped; short-sleeved.

NAME	Keith	Sue	John	Alexandra	Jane
AGE					
MARRIED?					
CHILDREN?					
JOB					
HEIGHT					
HAIR					
BUILD					
CLOTHES					

2 Can you put the right names with the photos?

3 Now listen to the recording of the five people talking. Try to note down the answers to the following questions.

1. What hours does Keith work?
2. How often does he go to church?
3. How does Sue get to work?
4. What does she like doing?
5. How old is John's daughter?
6. Does John like gardening?
7. How much does he say he drinks?
8. Does Alexandra read history books?
9. What newspaper does she read?
10. How many hours a week does Jane work?
11. What does Jane not like reading?
12. Two of the five people are married to each other. Which two?

Before you start, make sure you understand these words and expressions.

> antiques   cycling   darning socks   decorating
> history   historical novel   mending   philosophy
> science fiction   thriller
> Dick Francis (a popular thriller writer)
>
> Newspapers: *The Express*   *The Sun*
> *The Times*   *The Sunday Times*   *The Telegraph*

4 How do you feel about each of the five people? Do you find them interesting or not? Intelligent or not? Shy or self-confident? Do you like or dislike them? Which one would you most like to meet? Which one would you least like to meet?

5 Pronunciation. Listen to the recording. How many words do you hear in each sentence? What are they? (Contractions like *I'm* count as two words.)

6 Work in pairs. Look at your partner carefully for one minute. Then close your eyes (or turn your back) and say what he or she looks like, and what he or she is wearing Useful structures. *He/she has got...* *He/she is wearing...* Examples:

'*He's got dark brown hair.*'
'*She's wearing a light green blouse and black trousers.*'

7 *Is* or *has*?

1. She's 37.
2. What's he done?
3. It's late.
4. He's 1m 85 tall.
5. She's got blue eyes.
6. He's wearing a dark suit.
7. She's hungry.
8. He's cold.
9. She's gone to London.
10. He's married.
11. What colour's your new car?
12. She's tired.

8 Do you like or dislike these things? Write them in order of preference. Then see if anybody else in the class has put them in the same order.

> maths   dancing   dogs   snakes   babies
> cooking   shopping   chocolate

Now complete the table.

I very much like ....
....
....

I quite like ....
....
....

I don't mind ....
....
....

I don't much like ....
....
....

I can't stand ....
....
....

9 Study the Summary on page 134.

Other worlds

A There's a strange light in the sky

1 Look at the pictures and listen to the commentary. There are some differences. What are they?

2 How well can you remember the commentary? Complete the commentator's sentences.

1. 'Everybody .... up.'
2. 'The light .... from a strange machine.'
3. 'A door .... in the top.'
4. 'A strange thing .... out.'
5. 'They .... green suits.'
6. 'Now they .... across the field.'
7. 'He .... him over to the spaceship.'
8. 'He .... him inside.'
9. 'I .... down to have a word with our visitors.'
10. 'It .... out a gun.'
11. 'It .... it at me.'

3 Pronunciation. Listen to each word, and say whether you think it comes in the commentary or not. Examples:

eat / No.
it / Yes.
green / I think so.
filled / I don't think so.

4 Pronunciation. Listen to the recording. Do you hear A or B?

A	B
eat	it
green	grin
sheep	ship
field	filled

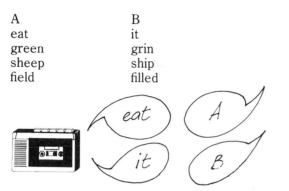

Listen to the recording and say whether the words are the same or different. Examples:

green, green — The same.

eat, it — Different.

Now say these words.

machine green field people believe dream

in picture listen difference is coming thing him ship inside visitor think

5 You are the commentator. The strange creatures have taken you away with Evans in the spaceship. You still have your portable radio transmitter, and you go on sending messages to Earth to tell people what is happening.

Look at the pictures below, and work with other students to prepare a commentary. Make the commentary different from the pictures in four or five places.

Give your commentary, and see if the class can find the differences.

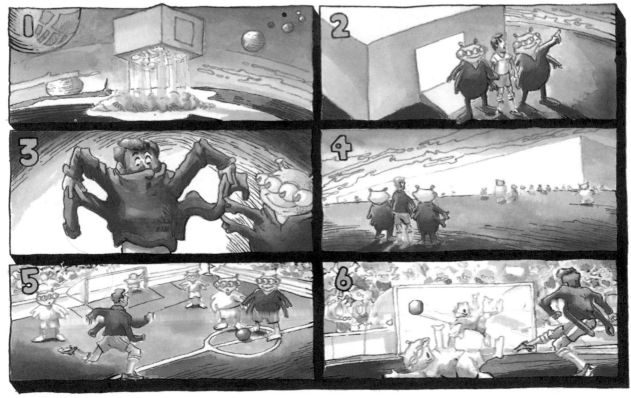

6 Study the Summary on page 135.

B What do you believe in?

1 **What do you believe in?**
a. Read the questions and choose your answers from the box. Write them down.
b. Work with another student. Guess how he or she has answered the questions, and write down your guesses. Then talk to your partner and find out if you were right.

1. Do you think that there may be intelligent life somewhere else in the universe?
2. Do you believe in 'flying saucers' (UFOs)?
3. Do you believe in ghosts (dead people who come back)?
4. Do you believe in reincarnation?
5. Do you believe in life after death?
6. Do you believe in a god?
7. Do you believe in telepathy?
8. Do you believe in horoscopes?
9. Do you think that some people can predict the future?
10. Do you think that we can learn important things from dreams?
11. Have you ever had experiences that you could not explain?

Possible answers:

'Yes, I do.'   'No, I don't.'
'Yes, I have.'   'No, I haven't.'
'Definitely (not).'   'Of course (not).'
'I'm not sure.'

---

2 **Listen to the recording and fill in the table. For each subject, write ✓ if the speaker believes in it, ✗ if he does not believe in it, and ？ if he is not sure.**

UFOs	
Life on other worlds	
Reincarnation	
Life after death	
Horoscopes	
Ghosts	

3 **Pronunciation. Say these words.**

believe   dream
in   think   thing   intelligent   predict

Now say these words and expressions.

thing   think   telepathy   death   I think there
that   the
there may be
I think that there may be
I think that there may be intelligent life in the universe.
I think that we can
I think that we can learn things from dreams.

12

4 Discussion. Work in groups of four or five. Talk about your answers to Exercise 1. Did you have more or fewer 'yes' answers than the others? Try to give reasons for some of your beliefs. Ask the teacher for help with vocabulary if necessary.

Useful expressions:

I agree with you.　　　　　Definitely not.
I don't agree.　　　　　　Yes and no.
I think you're right.　　　Nonsense!
Definitely.　　　　　　　Rubbish!

Language Study

5 Grammar revision. Compare these pairs of sentences.

They're walking across the field.
They usually walk to work.

The light's coming from a strange machine.
Our light comes from the sun.

What are you drinking?
Do you ever drink beer?

What is the difference between *they are walking* and *they walk*; *it is coming* and *it comes*; *are you drinking* and *do you drink*?

6 Choose the correct verb forms.

1. He *is smoking / smokes* 20 cigarettes a day.
2. What *are you looking / do you look* at?
3. 'Excuse me. *Are you speaking / Do you speak* French?' 'No, but I *'m speaking / speak* a little Spanish.'
4. 'Come and have a drink.' 'I'm sorry, I can't just now. I *'m working / work.'*
5. 'Why *are you driving / do you drive* so fast?' 'Because we're late.'
6. I *'m going / go* dancing every Friday night.
7. '*Do you often travel / 'Are you often travelling* abroad?' 'Four or five times a year.'
8. *Do you spell / Are you spelling* your name with one *n* or two?
9. 'What *are you thinking / do you think* about?' 'I'm not going to tell you.'
10. Water *is boiling / boils* at 100° Centigrade.
11. Can I turn off the TV? You *aren't watching / don't watch* it.

7 The same or different? You will hear ten pairs of words. If the two words in a pair are the same, write 'S'. If they are different, write 'D'.

8 Pronunciation. Can you hear a *th?*
Circle the words you hear.

1. mouth / mouse
2. thin / sin
3. thought / taught
4. thanks / tanks
5. there / dare
6. bathe / bays
7. they / day

9 Test other students. Say one of the words from Exercise 8. The other students have to say Yes if they hear a *th*.

10 Study the Summary on page 135–136.

The past

A A true story

1 Listen to the recording without looking at the text, and see how much of the story you can understand.

2 Read the text and fill in the gaps with words from the boxes.

ESCAPE FROM THE JUNGLE
(This is a true story.)

On Christmas Eve 1971 Juliana Koepke, a seventeen-year-old German girl, ... Lima by air with her mother. They .... on their way to Pucallpa, another town in Peru, to spend Christmas with Juliana's father. Forty-five minutes later the plane .... up in a storm, and Juliana .... 3,000 metres, strapped in her seat. She was not killed when the seat .... the ground (perhaps because trees broke her fall), but she .... all night unconscious.

The next morning Juliana .... for pieces of the plane, and .... for her mother. Nobody answered, and she .... nothing except a small plastic bag of sweets.

Juliana's collar bone was broken, one knee was badly hurt and she had deep cuts on her arms and legs. She had no shoes; her glasses were broken (so she could not .... snakes or spiders, for example); and she was wearing only a very short dress, which was badly torn. But she decided to try to .... out of the jungle, because she .... that if she stayed there she would die.

So Juliana .... to walk. She did not .... anything to eat, and as the days went by she got weaker and weaker. She was also in bad trouble from insect bites. She .... helicopters, but could not see them above the trees, and of course they could not see her. One day she .... three seats and .... that they had dead bodies in them, but she did not recognise the people.

After four days she .... to a river. She saw caimans and piranhas, but she .... that they do not usually attack people. So Juliana walked and .... down the river for another five days. At last she .... to a hut. Nobody was there, but the next afternoon, four men arrived. They .... her to a doctor in the next village.

Juliana .... afterwards that there were at least three other people who were not killed in the crash. But she was the only one who .... out of the jungle. It took her ten days.

Put the correct forms of these verbs into the gaps marked   .

be   break   call   fall
find   hit   leave   lie   look

Put the correct forms of these verbs into the gaps marked   .

find   find   get   hear
know   see   see   start

Put the correct forms of these verbs into the gaps marked   .

come   come   get
know   learn   swim   take

sweets   snake   spider   piranha   caiman   hut   helicopter

5 Prepare five questions about the text. Example:

'When did Juliana leave Lima?'

When you are ready, work with another student. Close your book. Ask your questions, and answer your partner's.
If you have problems understanding each other, use these sentences to help you.

'Sorry, could you say that again?'
'I'm sorry, I don't understand.'
'What do you mean?'

If you can't answer a question, say:

'Sorry, I don't know.'
'I'm afraid I can't remember.'

6 Pronunciation. Copy these words. Then listen to the recording and circle the words you hear.

1. works / worked
2. rains / rained
3. starting / started
4. There's / There was
5. smells / smelt
6. stops / stopped
7. There's / There was
8. try / tried
9. puts / put
10. using / uses

3 Can you remember what you read? Close your book, listen to the recording, and write 'S' ('the same') or 'D' ('different') for each sentence.

4 Put in the correct forms.

1. How did Juliana *leave / left* Lima?
2. She *leave / left* by air.
3. How far did Juliana *fall / fell*?
4. She *fall / fell* 3,000 metres.
5. What did Juliana *look / looked* for?
6. She *look / looked* for pieces of the plane.

7 Work in groups of five or six. Tell other students about a bad day in your life.

8 Study the Summary on page 136.

B Did you have a good day?

1 Listen to the conversation with your book closed. Who did Lorna talk to during the day?

GEORGE: Hello, darling. Did you have a good day?

LORNA: Not bad. The usual sort of thing. Meetings, phone calls, letters. You know.

GEORGE: Did you see anybody interesting?

LORNA: Well, Chris came into the office this morning. We had a long talk.

GEORGE: Oh, yes? What about?

LORNA: Oh, this and that. Things. You know.

GEORGE: I see.

LORNA: And then Janet turned up. As usual. Just when I was trying to finish some work.

GEORGE: So what did you do?

LORNA: Had lunch with her.

GEORGE: Where did you go? Somewhere nice?

LORNA: No. Just the pub round the corner. A pie and a pint, you know. Then in the afternoon there was a budget meeting. It went on for hours.

GEORGE: Sounds like a boring day. Did anything interesting happen?

LORNA: Don't think so, not really. Can't remember. Oh, yes, one thing. Something rather strange.

GEORGE: What?

LORNA: Well, it was this evening. I was getting ready to come home. And the phone rang. So I picked it up. And there was this man.

GEORGE: Who?

LORNA: Well, I don't know. He wouldn't say who he was. But he asked me to have lunch with him tomorrow.

GEORGE: What?

LORNA: Yes. He said he wanted to talk to me. About something very important.

GEORGE: So what did you say?

LORNA: Well, I said yes, of course. How was your day?

2 Look at this sentence.

Had lunch with her.

Lorna leaves out the pronoun *I*. Can you find any more sentences where Lorna leaves out words?

3 Now listen again to George's side of the conversation with your book closed. Can you remember the beginnings of Lorna's answers?

4 Pronunciation: the letter *a*. Can you pronounce these words?

1. bad   had   happen   rang   man   (/æ/)
2. darling   afternoon   rather   ask   glass   (/ɑ:/)
3. came   strange   day   say   train (/eɪ/)
4. call   talk   saw   (/ɔ:/)

Put these words in group 1, 2, 3 or 4.

wait   hate   hard   glass   start   law   car
bath   late   ball   black   make   paid   arm
rain   fall   hat   part   happy   half   past
awful   may   all   stand   walk

Special pronunciations:

what   wasn't   want   watch   swan   (/ɒ/)
many   any   again   says   said   ate   (/e/)
about   America   England   umbrella   (/ə/)

5 Grammar: simple past and past progressive. Study the examples.

> *Just when I* **was trying** *to finish some work*
>
> Janet
> **turned** *up*.
>
> *I* **was getting** *ready to come home*
>
> and the
> phone **rang**.

Now put the correct verb forms into the sentences.

1. Andrew .... when I was getting ready to go out. (*arrive*)
2. The phone rang while I .... a bath. (*have*)
3. I first met my wife when I .... in Berlin. (*study*)
4. When I looked out of the window, it .... (*rain*)
5. I stopped because the car .... a funny noise. (*make*)
6. Where were you going when I .... you yesterday? (*see*)
7. When I was cleaning the house, I .... some old love letters. (*find*)
8. The accident .... while we .... into Copenhagen. (*happen; drive*)
9. I .... all my money when I .... from Istanbul to Athens. (*lose; travel*)
10. When I .... her, she .... reading. (*see; sit*)
11. The lights all .... while we .... supper. (*go out; have*)
12. When I .... the train, I .... my ticket onto the railway line. (*get off; drop*)

6 Imagine that it is six o'clock in the evening. You have just arrived home after an interesting day. What did you do? Make up answers to the following questions (ask the teacher for help if necessary).

What is your job?
How did you spend the morning?
Where did you have lunch? What did you have?
How did you spend the afternoon?
What places did you go to? Why?
You saw somebody interesting during the day. Who? When did you meet? ('*When I was ...ing.*') What did you talk about? What did you do together?
Something interesting or strange happened during the day. What? When did it happen? ('*When I was ...ing.*')

7 Work in pairs. You and your partner are members of the same family, or husband and wife, or flatmates or roommates in college. Talk about how you both spent your day (using the ideas from Exercise 6).
Useful expressions:

Did you have a good day?
Did you see anybody interesting?
What about?
You know.
I see.
as usual
So what did you do?
Where did you go?
What did you say?
What happened then?
Did anything interesting happen?
Not really.
(It) sounds like a boring/interesting day.

8 Work in groups. Tell the group what you did yesterday; or tell them about your last holiday; or about a journey that you made once; or about your earliest memory.

9 Study the Summary on page 137.

Comparisons

A Things are different

1 Look at the pictures. How many differences can you find between them?
Example: *'The fridge is bigger in picture B.'*

A   B

2 Revision. *-er* or *more*?

Examples: tall ....*taller*........

important *more important*

old   interesting   beautiful   long   short
difficult   small   easy   cheap   expensive

-est or *most*?

Examples: tall ....*tallest*........

important *most important*

fast   heavy   surprising   cheerful   boring
nice   young   light   intelligent   hard

3 Copy the table. Then listen and fill in the gaps.

	A	B	C	D	E	F
Number of wheels	4					
How many people does it carry?						1
Top speed (in kph)						
Weight (in kilos)						
Price (in pounds)						

4 What are A, B, C, D, E and F? Choose the correct vehicles.

ship   plane   car   bus   lorry   tank   pram
train   motorbike   bicycle

5 Complete these sentences.

1. E has got *the most* wheels.
2. C and F have got *the fewest* wheels.
3. E can carry .... people.
4. F can carry .... people.
5. .... is the fastest.
6. A is the ....
7. .... is the lightest.
8. E ....
9. E .... expensive.
10. .... cheapest.

6 Listen to the recording. How many words do you hear in each sentence? (Contractions like *she's* count as two words.)

7 Look at the table and make some sentences (some true, some false). Ask other students if they are true or false. Use these structures:

...... has got more wheels than ....
...... hasn't got as many wheels as ....
...... can carry (far) more people than ....
...... can't carry (nearly) as many people
     as ....
...... is (much) faster/heavier than ....
...... costs (much) more than ....
...... doesn't cost (nearly) as much as ....
     (OR: ...... costs much less than ....)
...... has got the most/fewest ....
...... can carry the most/fewest ....
...... is the fastest/slowest/heaviest/etc.

8 Choose one of these groups of things. Ask other students which of the things in the group they would most like to have, and why. Ask as many people as possible, and write down the answers.

1. a dog   a cat   a horse   a bird
2. a Rolls Royce   a Citroen 2CV   a motorbike
   a bicycle
3. a piano   a guitar   a violin   a trumpet
4. a holiday in the mountains / by the sea /
   in London / in San Francisco
5. a flat   a cottage   a big house
6. more money   more intelligence
   more free time   more friends

9 Tell the class what you found out in Exercise 8. Example:

'I asked about Group 1. Most people would prefer a bird, because it doesn't eat as much as the others.'
(OR: '. . . it eats less than the others.')

B People are different

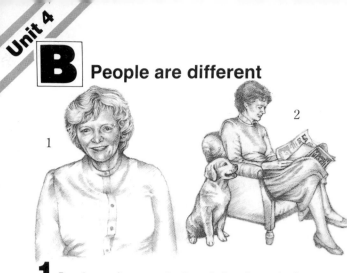

1 Look at pictures 1–6 and the descriptions. Can you put the right name with each picture?

ANN is a dark-haired woman who is rather shy.
LESLIE is a young doctor who plays tennis.
SUSAN is a fair-haired woman who speaks French.
PAT is a company director who eats too much.
KATE is a fair-haired woman who does not smoke.
CAROL is a dark-haired woman who likes animals.

2 Now look at pictures 7–12. Make up names and descriptions for the people in them. (Use *who* in your sentences.) Then see if other students can put your names with the right pictures.

3 Go round the class, and see how many of these people you can find in five minutes. Write down their names when you find them. Prepare your questions first. Examples:

'*Do you like fish?*'
'*When were you born?*'

FIND:

somebody who doesn't like fish.
somebody who was born in June.
somebody who has been to New York.
somebody who likes maths.
somebody who believes in horoscopes.
somebody who can't swim.
somebody who has got a cold.
somebody who hates pop music.
somebody who often has bad dreams.
somebody who has got a headache.
somebody who is very shy.
somebody who is not shy at all.

4 Listen to the recording, and decide whether the following sentences are true or false.

1. Keith is much taller than John.
2. Keith and John are both slim.
3. They both like gardening.
4. Keith's hair is darker than John's.
5. Keith has some sort of dressing in his hair.
6. John's face is thinner than Keith's.
7. Keith is wearing a black striped T-shirt.
8. John is wearing black shoes.
9. John is wearing black socks.

5 Pronunciation. Say these sentences. Pay attention to stress, rhythm and linking.

1. My **bro**ther and **I** are **ve**ry **dif**ferent.
2. He's **not nearly as old** as **me**.
3. He's **much taller** than **me**.
4. His **in**terests are **dif**ferent from **mine**.
5. He **looks like** our father, but **I look like** our **mo**ther.
6. He **likes foot**ball, but **I don't**.
7. He **en**joys **par**ties **much more** than **I do**.
8. He's **in**terested in com**pu**ters, but **I'm** not.
9. My **sis**ter and **I** are **quite si**milar.
10. We **both have fair hair**, and we are **both left-han**ded.
11. Her **eyes** are the **same co**lour as **mine**.
12. We **both play** the piano.
13. She **sings be**tter than **I do**.
14. We were **both born** in Sep**tem**ber.
15. She **likes tra**velling, but **I don't**.
16. **Both** of us **play ten**nis.
17. **Nei**ther of us can **swim**.
18. She is a **bit taller** than **me**.
19. We are **both ra**ther **shy**, and we **both like li**ving alone.

"Got any S shirts?"

6 A person with dark hair is *dark-haired*. Somebody who writes with his or her left hand is *left-handed*. What are the adjectives for these people?

1. a person with brown hair
2. somebody with blue eyes
3. a person who has broad shoulders
4. people who write with their right hands
5. a person with a thin face
6. somebody with long legs

Now say these in another way.

1. a blue-eyed girl
   'a girl with blue eyes'
2. a brown-haired man
   'a man ...'
3. a left-handed child
   'a child who ...'
4. a fat-faced person
   'somebody who has ...'
5. a dark-eyed woman
   '...'
6. a long-sleeved pullover
   '... with ...'

7 Work with a student that you don't know very well. Write down three ways in which you think you are different from your partner, and three ways in which you think you are similar. Then exchange your papers and discuss what you wrote. Were you right?

8 Now find out more about your partner. Try to find at least five things that you have in common, and at least five differences, and write them down. Use some of the language from Exercise 5; ask your teacher for words you don't know.
Useful expressions:

'Do you mind if I ask you a personal question?'
'No, that's all right.'

'How old are you?'
'I would rather not answer.'

Asking and offering

A Have you got some stuff for cleaning windows?

1 Vocabulary revision. Where do you buy these things?

meat bread vegetables sugar shoes
soap books clothes writing paper petrol
stamps aspirin films

Example:

'You buy sugar at a grocer's or at a supermarket.'

2 Look at the conversations and try to fill in some of the gaps. Then listen to the recording and write the complete conversations.

1. 'Good afternoon.'
   'Hello. .... a shampoo for dry hair.'
   'Large, medium or ....?'
   '..................... the small bottle?'
   '76p.'
   '..................... two bottles, please.'

2. '.....................?'
   'Yes, ...'

3. 'Can I help you?'
   '..................... I'm being served.'

4. '.....................?'
   '..................... a child's tricycle.'
   'Yes. .... the child?'

5. '..................... a pint of milk, please?'
   'Yes, of course.......................
   ....?'
   'No, ..., thanks.
   ....?'
   '24p.'

6. 'Hello, Sid. .... any flashbulbs?'
   'I'm afraid not, Fred. ....
   some in next week. Can you look in on Monday?'
   '..................... be away on Monday, but I'll call in on Tuesday.'
   'OK. ....'
   'Bye, Sid.'

7. '..................... a dishwasher.'
   '............. .... make?'
   '..................... Kleenwash XJ126?'
   'Yes, we have. It's a very good machine.'
   '..................... guarantee?'
   'Five years, madam.'
   '..................... deliver?'
   'Yes, we do, sir. Up to 20 miles.'
   'How much is it?'
   '....................., plus VAT.'

3 Rhythm and stress. Say these expressions.

Good **after**noon.
I'm **being served**.
a **pint** of **milk**
a **child's tri**cycle
Yes, we **have**.
Yes, of **course**.
Here you **are**.
I'm a**fraid not**.
the **small bot**tle
How much is the **small bot**tle?
How much is it?
How old is the **child**?
It's a **very good** ma**chine**.

4 Dialogue practice. Work with a partner and practise one or more of the conversations from Exercise 2.

5 Here are some ways to ask for things when you don't know the word.

Useful words:		
a thing	stuff	square
a machine	liquid	round
a tool	powder	
	material	

Useful structures:
a thing **with** a hole / **with** a handle

a machine **for making** holes
a tool **for cutting** wood
a thing **for putting** pieces of paper together

some material **for making** curtains
some liquid **for cleaning** windows
some powder **for washing** clothes
some stuff **for killing** insects

Example:
A: Excuse me. I don't speak English very well. What do you call the round glass in a camera?
B: The lens.
A: The lens. OK. I need some material for cleaning the lens.
B: A lens cleaner. Yes, we have …

Now look at the pictures and ask for one of the things illustrated.

6 Dramatisation. Work in pairs or groups of three. Prepare and practise conversations in shops. Use some of the expressions from Exercises 2 and 5.

B I haven't got anything to wear

1 Read the conversation and then listen to the recording. How many differences can you find?

JAN: Hello, Kate. What's the matter?

KATE: Hello, Jan. Oh, dear. I'm going out with Tony tonight, and I haven't got anything to wear.

JAN: What about your blue dress? That's lovely.

KATE: That old thing? No. It makes me look like a sack of potatoes.

JAN: Well, why don't you borrow something of mine?

KATE: Could I really?

JAN: Yes, of course. Would you like to?

KATE: Well, I'd love to. If you really don't mind.

JAN: What about that green silk thing?

KATE: Green silk?

JAN: Yes, you know. The dress I wore to Andy's birthday party.

KATE: Oh, yes. I remember.

JAN: You'd look great in that.

KATE: Oooh!

JAN: And I'll lend you my new shoes to go with it.

KATE: My feet are bigger than yours.

JAN: I don't think they are, Kate. Anyway, try the shoes and see. What about a jacket? Have you got one that will do?

KATE: Not really.

JAN: Well. have one of mine.

KATE: Oh, Jan. I feel bad, borrowing all your things.

JAN: That's all right. What are friends for? I'll borrow something of yours one of these days.

KATE: Well, thanks a million, Jan. I'd better get moving. Tony's coming in half an hour.

JAN: OK. Wait a second. I'll go and get the dress. Shall I iron it for you?

KATE: Oh, Jan, . . .

2 Match the questions and answers.

1. Can you lend me some stamps?
2. Excuse me. Have you got the time?
3. Can I borrow your pen?
4. Could you help me for a few minutes?
5. Have you got a light?
6. Shall I post these letters for you?
7. Could I borrow your bicycle for half an hour?
8. Have you got change for £1?
9. Could I use your phone?
10. Would you like to play tennis this evening?
11. Excuse me. Can you tell me the way to the station?
12. I'll give you a hand with the cooking, shall I?

a. Sorry, I don't smoke.
b. I think so. How many do you need?
c. Sorry, I'm afraid I'm using it.
d. Sorry, I'm not free. My son's coming round.
e. Just after half past three.
f. Perhaps – I'll have a look. Yes, here you are.
g. OK. Can you put it back on my desk when you've finished with it?
h. That's very kind of you. Could you do the potatoes?
i. Well, I'm in a bit of a hurry.
j. Of course. It's over there on the table.
k. Sorry, I'm a stranger here myself.
l. Yes, please, if you don't mind.

3 Pronunciation. Which words do you hear?

A	B	A	B
sale	sell	paper	pepper
late	let	pain	pen
gate	get	whale	well
main	men	wait	wet

Now pronounce some of the words yourself. Ask other students which words they think you are saying.

4 Pronunciation and spelling. Say these words.

1. Kate change table strange make
2. day way play
3. wait chain fail
4. station pronunciation

Can you think of any more words to put into groups 1, 2, 3 and 4?

5 Grammar. Infinitive with or without *to*?

1. I haven't got anything *to eat / eat*.
2. Why don't you *to take / take* a holiday?
3. I would like *to go / go* out tonight.
4. 'That's the doorbell.' 'I'll *to go / go*.'
5. Can you *to lend / lend* me some money?
6. That dress makes her *to look / look* funny.
7. I hope *to see / see* you again soon.
8. Shall I *to carry / carry* that bag for you?
9. What time do you have *to start / start* work in the mornings?
10. It's nice *to see / see* you again.

6 Ask other students if you can borrow things from them. Use questions and answers from Exercise 2.

7 Write two or more notes to other students. In your notes, you must ask somebody for something, offer something to somebody, or offer to do something for somebody. Answer the notes that you get. Use words and expressions from Exercises 1 and 2.

Dear Anne,
Could I borrow your bike this evening? Yours, Patricia

Dear Pat,
Of course you can, I'll give it to you after the lesson.
Anne

Dear Tony,
Shall I drive you to the airport on Saturday?
Love,
Alice

Dear Alice,
Thank you very much. That's very kind of you. My plane's at 11.30.
Love,
T.

The future

A Their children will have blue eyes

1 How much do you know about genetics? See if you can complete the sentences correctly. When you have finished, ask the teacher for the answers.

1. If both parents have got blue eyes, their children:
   will certainly have blue eyes.
   will probably have blue eyes.
   may have blue eyes.
2. If both parents have got brown eyes, their children:
   will certainly have brown eyes.
   will probably have brown eyes.
   may have brown eyes.
3. If one parent has got blue eyes and one has got brown eyes, their children:
   will certainly have blue eyes.
   will probably have blue eyes.
   may have blue eyes or brown eyes.
   will probably have brown eyes.
   will certainly have brown eyes.
4. If a man (but not his wife) is colour-blind, their daughters:
   will be colour-blind.
   may be colour-blind.
   will probably not be colour-blind.
   will almost certainly not be colour-blind.
5. If a man (but not his wife) is colour-blind, their sons:
   will certainly be colour-blind.
   may be colour-blind.
   will probably not be colour-blind.
   will certainly not be colour-blind.

2 Look at the picture. The couple are going to have a baby. What do you think it will be like? Make sentences beginning *It will ...* or *It may ...*

3 Pronunciation. Say these words and expressions.

know   so   go   hope   don't   won't
I know   I hope   I won't
I don't know   I hope so   I won't go

Now say these words and expressions.

will   I'll   you'll   he'll   she'll
I'll tell   I'll think   you'll be
she'll have   it'll rain
I'll tell you tomorrow   I'll think about it
You'll be sorry   She'll have to go soon
Do you think it'll rain tonight?

Carol works in a computer firm. She is rather shy, and often gets depressed. She is not very interested in sport, but she likes playing tennis. She is very musical, and can play several instruments.

Lee is a bus driver. He is a very sociable, outgoing person, optimistic and cheerful. He likes sport, especially ball games. He is interested in science, and he is studying maths at night school. He is not at all musical.

4 What will your children be like? (If you already have children, talk about your grandchildren. If you're not going to have children, talk about somebody else's children.) Use *will, won't, may. I (don't) think, I hope.* Examples:

'I hope my children will be good-looking.'
'My children may be musical.'
'I don't think my children will be tall.'
'My children certainly won't speak English.'

5 What sort of world will your great-grandchildren live in? Make some sentences.

In 70 years, people

may
will

(not)

be able to
have to

go to the moon for the weekend.
shop by computer.
work.
drive cars.
travel where they like.
speak Chinese.
etc.

6 The difference between *will* and *is going to.* Compare:

She **is going to** have a baby.
The baby **will** have blue eyes, and it **will** probably have fair hair.
She hopes it **will** be a girl.

Now study this rule. Use a dictionary to help you if necessary.

– We use *am/are/is going to* when we can already see the future in the present – when future actions are already planned, or are beginning to happen.
– We use *will* when we predict future actions by thinking, hoping, or calculating.

7 Look at the pictures and say what is going to happen.

8 *Will* or *going to?*

1. Look out! *We'll / We're going to* crash!
2. I hope one day *I'll / I'm going to* have more free time.
3. *Mary'll / Mary's going to* marry an old friend of mine in August.
4. I can't talk to you now. *We'll just / We're just going to* have lunch.
5. Perhaps in a few hundred years everybody *will / is going to* have an easy life.
6. 'What are your plans for this evening?'
   'I'll / I'm going to stay at home and watch TV.'
7. 'John's starting university in October.'
   'Oh, yes? *What will he / What's he going to* study?'
8. If you and your husband both have green eyes, your children *will probably / are probably going to* have green eyes too.

9 What are your plans for this evening / tomorrow / the weekend? Examples:

'This evening I'm going to stay in and wash my hair.'
'We're going to spend the weekend in the mountains.'

B How about Thursday?

1 Here are the beginnings and ends of three conversations. Which beginning goes with which end?

A

'Parkhurst 7298.'
'Hello. Paul?'
'Hello. Who's that?'
'This is Audrey. I wondered if you were free .... Tuesday.'
'It depends. What time?'
'............ the afternoon?'
'Yes, I could be. Why?'
'Well, my mother's coming down, and I'd like you to meet her. About half past four?'

B

'Hello, John. This is Angela. I'm trying to fix the Directors' meeting. Can you tell me what days you're free next week?'
'Well, let me see. Monday morning's OK. Tuesday. Not Wednesday, I'm going to Cardiff. Thursday afternoon. Friday's a bit difficult.'
'How about Thursday two fifteen?'

C

'Hello. I'd like to make an appointment to see Dr Gray.'
'Yes. What name is it, please?'
'Simon Graftey.'
'Yes. Three o'clock .... Monday, Mr Graftey?'
'Three o'clock's difficult. Could it be earlier?'

D

'Tuesday two fifteen. Let me look in my diary.'
'No, Thursday.'
'Oh, I'm sorry, I thought you said Tuesday. Thursday two fifteen. No, I'm sorry, I've got an appointment until three. Could we make it later? Say three fifteen?'
'Well, there's a lot to talk about. It'll take a couple of hours, at least.'
'Shall we say Monday morning, then?'
'Monday morning. All right. Nine o'clock?'
'Nine. I think that's all right. I'll ring you back and confirm.'
'All right. But ring .... five, could you?'
'I'll call you back .... about half an hour, Angela. All right?'
'Right you are. Bye, John.'
'Bye.'

E

'Two thirty?'
'No, I'm afraid I can't manage two thirty either. I'm seeing somebody .... two forty. Is two o'clock possible?'
'Yes, that's all right. Two o'clock .... Monday, then.'
'Thanks very much. Goodbye.'
'Goodbye.'

F

'That's difficult. You see, I'm playing tennis .... a quarter past. Then it'll take me a few minutes to shower and get changed.'
'What about later? Say, five?'
'Yes, OK. I'll come round .... five. Your place?'
'My place.'
'OK. See you then. Bye.'
'Bye.'

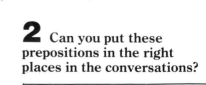

2 Can you put these prepositions in the right places in the conversations?

at	at	in	in	on	on
on	before	until			

28

3 Listen to the conversations. Then look at the text and see how these words and structures are used. Ask your teacher for explanations if necessary.

1. Present progressive tense with future meaning (e.g. *My mother's coming down*).
2. *How about . . . ?* and *Shall we . . . ?* in suggestions.
3. *I'd like to . . .*
4. *I'll . . .* in promises.

Write down ten more useful words, expressions or structures to learn. Can you find any other students who have chosen the same expressions as you?

4 How many stresses? Where are they? Listen to the recording to check your answers.

I wondered if you were free on Tuesday. (3)
In the afternoon?
I'd like you to meet her.
I'm trying to fix the Directors' meeting.
Can you tell me what days you're free...
Friday's a bit difficult.
I'd like to make an appointment...
There's a lot to talk about.
It'll take a couple of hours...
I'll call you back in about half an hour...
I'm playing tennis until a quarter past.

5 Practise one of the conversations with another student.

6 Fill in your diary for Saturday and Sunday. Put in at least eight of the following activities (and any others that you want to add), but leave yourself some free time.

wash your hair   write to your mother
play tennis   buy a sweater   see a film
have a drink with a friend   go to a party
clean the kitchen   mend some clothes
practise the guitar   study English grammar
make a cake   do your ironing   wash the car
go to church   go and see your sister
do some gardening

SATURDAY
9.00 clean kitchen
12.00 shop. Buy sweater
Lunch with Sally.
Afternoon Tennis
5.00 Guitar lesson.

SUNDAY
Morning: Wash hair and mend clothes
12.30 Drink with Carl
Afternoon — Write to mother.
Party.

HELLO, ANN. ARE YOU FREE ON SUNDAY?

IT DEPENDS. WHAT TIME?

ABOUT THREE O'CLOCK?

THAT'S DIFFICULT. I'M PLAYING TENNIS. WHAT ABOUT LATER?

7 'Telephone' another student. Try to arrange to do something together at the weekend.

Things that have happened

A Have you ever...?

1 Listen to the song. You will hear it twice. The second time, try to remember the words that have been left out.

2 Ask and answer questions beginning *Have you ever eaten / seen / climbed / met / been to / broken /...?* etc. Example:

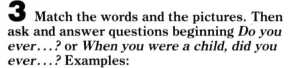

HAVE YOU EVER EATEN OCTOPUS?

NO, I NEVER HAVE.

YES. I EAT IT EVERY DAY.

NO, BUT I'VE EATEN SHARK.

YES, I ATE SOME LAST SUMMER.

YES, I'VE EATEN IT TWICE.

3 Match the words and the pictures. Then ask and answer questions beginning *Do you ever...?* or *When you were a child, did you ever...?* Examples:

'*Do you ever go walking in the rain?*'
'*When you were a child, did you ever go camping?*'

1. refuse to take medicine
2. stay up all night reading
3. dream of being someone else
4. take part in demonstrations
5. go out alone
6. want to be taller or shorter

One please.

4 What are the differences between *Have you ever...?*, *Do you ever...?* and *Did you ever...?*

5 Choose the correct tense (present, present perfect or past).

1. When you were a child, *have you ever run / did you ever run* away from home?
2. My brother *has had / had* a fight with his neighbour last week.
3. *Do you ever / Did you ever* travel by boat?
4. *Have you ever broken / Did you ever break* your ankle?
5. I *have often dreamt / often dreamt* of having a billion dollars.
6. During the last three years, I *have travelled / travelled* about 100,000 miles.
7. 'Do you know Canada?' 'No, *I've never been / I never went* there.'
8. I've got a very interesting job, and I *meet / met* lots of famous people.
9. I *haven't liked / didn't like* grammar at school, but I'm very interested in it now.
10. *I've spoken / I spoke* to the President several times.
11. *Have you ever / Did you ever* put an advertisement in a newspaper?
12. When we were small, Mother *has made / made* us delicious ice-cream every Sunday.

6 Listen to some people talking about past experiences. For each experience put a ✓ if they have had it, and a ✗ if they have not.

	1	2	3	4
eating snails				
going to America				
spending more than a day in hospital				
running a mile				

Now listen again. Try to pick out these words, and write down the verbs that go with them.

quite often   twice   very often
never   ever   recently   on one occasion
before   now

7 In groups of three or four, make a list of ten or more questions that you can ask about someone's life, interests, work, etc. Examples:

'Where did you live when you were a child?'
'Can you talk about two happy times in your life?'
'Have you ever studied music?'

8 Find a person from another group. Ask the questions that you have prepared (and other questions, too, if you like). Note the answers.

9 Write some sentences (about eight), using some of the information from Exercise 8. Don't use the person's name in your sentences.

10 Pass your sentences to the teacher, who will read them to the class. The class has to guess who the sentences are about.

"Fifteen years we've commuted together on this train; fifteen years all we've ever said to each other has been 'Good Morning' – I'd just like you to know, I love you."

31

B Here is the news

1 Complete these sentences and write them out correctly. (You may need to put more than one word in a blank.) To get the information you need, look at the statistics and the background information on Fantasia, and listen to the news broadcast.

1. The population of Fantasia has *doubled / trebled / quadrupled* since 1900.
2. The population of San Fantastico *increased / decreased / has increased / has decreased* since 1900.
3. Fantasia used to be highly industrialised, but now has a mainly agricultural economy. True or false?
4. The Fantasians .... to have parliamentary elections every .... years. Since 1980, they *have / had / have had* parliamentary elections every .... years.
5. Mrs Rask *is / was / has been* President of Fantasia for .... years.
6. Fantasia has just .... a .... of Friendship and Protection with Outland.
7. Outland .... be a Fantasian colony. It *became / has become* independent in ....
8. .... of Outland and his wife have just arrived in Fantasia for a state visit.
9. President Rask and Mrs Martin *know / knew / have known* each other .... a long time.
10. They *first met / have first met* at the Olympic Games in 19.., where Mrs Rask *won / has won* a silver medal for the high jump.
11. Dr Rask .... just .... from a trip abroad.
12. He has been visiting Third World countries for the last .... weeks in his capacity as President of 'Families .... '.
13. The percentage of homeless people in Fantasia has *risen / fallen* considerably .... 1900.
14. Unemployment figures .... *improved / worsened* since 1950.
15. The percentage of women in paid employment has *risen / fallen* .... 1950.
16. A fire .... burning .... three days in Grand South Station.
17. It .... raining steadily .... the last .... weeks in Fantasia, and the river Fant .... burst its banks.
18. The heavy rains have ruined some crops, and .... prices in San Fantastico .... going up steadily for the last .... days. The Minister for Consumer Affairs .... announced that price controls on vegetables and fruit will come into effect ....

FANTASIA: SOME STATISTICS

ITEM	1900	1950	TODAY
Population	20m	35m	60m
Population of San Fantastico	1.2m	4.3m	3.6m
Average number of children per family	4.5	3.6	2
Working week (hours)	54	49	42
Paid holiday (weeks per year)	0	2	5
Size of army	500,000	200,000	50,000
Homeless	23%	17%	8%
Unemployment	20%	7%	17%
Women in paid employment	18%	23%	79%
Percentage of workforce in agriculture	84%	66%	19%
Contribution of agriculture to Gross National Product	78%	51%	8%
Contribution of industry to Gross National Product	11%	38%	83%
Foreign tourists per year	?	30,000	6m

FANTASIA AND OUTLAND: SOME BACKGROUND INFORMATION

Since the revolution in 1886, Fantasia has been a parliamentary democracy. There are two Houses of Parliament: elections to both used to be held every seven years, but since the Electoral Reform Act of 1980, elections have been held every four years. The president is elected separately by popular vote; the last presidential election was held three years ago. Mrs Kirsten Rask, the current president, is a distinguished physicist. She is also a former Olympic athlete who won a silver medal for the high jump in the 1960 Games.

Outland was formerly the Fantasian colony of South Wesk, but has been independent since the end of the War of Independence in 1954. Relations between the two countries have become more friendly since Mrs Rask's election, and Fantasia has just signed a 'Treaty of Friendship and Protection' with Outland. President Martin of Outland was at university with the Fantasian president's husband, Dr Erasmus Rask, and Mrs Martin and Mrs Rask have been friends since they met at the 1960 Olympics.

2 **Look at the two pictures. What differences can you see? Examples:**

'*There used to be a church to the right of the bridge.*'
'*People's clothes have changed.*'
'*People didn't use to travel by car.*'

VIEW FROM WESK SQUARE AROUND 1890

VIEW FROM WESK SQUARE 1985

3 Grammar revision. Can you answer these questions?

1. A man says, 'I've been in France for six years'. Is he in France when he says this?
2. A woman says, 'I was in Japan for three years'. Is she in Japan when she says this?
3. Somebody says, 'I've worked with Eric for 30 years, and I worked with Sally for 25 years'. Which one does he still work with?
4. Somebody says, 'I did seven years' French at school'. Is he or she still at school?
5. You are in America. Somebody asks, 'How long are you here for?' Does the person want to know when your visit started, or when it will end?
6. What does 'How long have you been here for?' mean?

4 Grammar. Choose the correct form.

1. I *am writing* / *have been writing* / *wrote* letters for the last two hours.
2. I *am going* / *go* / *have been going* out with some friends tonight.
3. 'How long *are you learning* / *have you been learning* English?' 'Since last summer.'
4. When I was a child, we *have been living* / *have lived* / *lived* in a house by a river.
5. I *have had* / *have* this watch since my 18th birthday.
6. 'How long *have you known* / *do you know* Jessica?' 'We *have been* / *were* at school together 40 years ago.'
7. I *am* / *have been* ill for three days now. I think I'd better call the doctor.

5 Pronunciation. These words all have the letter *e* in the first syllable. In some of the words, *e* is pronounced /e/; in others, it is pronounced /ɪ/. Can you divide the words into two groups, according to the pronunciation of *e*? What is the reason for the difference?

become   depend
democracy   demonstration
economy   effect   election
employment   end   every
held   medal   president
reform   relations   return
revolution   secretary
separate   seven   vegetable

6 Work in groups. Prepare a short news item, with information about what has happened recently in your country, in the world, in your class, or in Fantasia.

Know before you go

A Going to Britain

1 Look through the text to find the answers to these questions.

1. How can you write *fifty pence* in another way?
2. Where can you usually get a good inexpensive meal?
3. Where can you ask about an inexpensive place to stay?
4. Is all medical care for foreigners free in Britain?
5. Which is cheaper, travelling by train or travelling by coach?

Money   There are one hundred pence (100p) in a pound (£1). People sometimes say 'p' instead of 'pence'; for example, 'eighty p'. Not all banks change foreign money, but you can usually find at least one bank in each town that will do so.

Where to stay   Hotels are very expensive in Britain. A cheaper solution is a 'bed and breakfast' in someone's home. Information centres or tourist offices can help you to find these. There are also youth hostels and campsites in many places.

Getting around   Trains are fairly good in Britain. If you are under 24 or over 65, or if you are travelling with a family, ask about 'railcards' for cheaper fares on the train. There are also coaches (long-distance buses) between some towns and cities; these are cheaper than trains. In towns and cities, there are usually buses, and in London there is also an underground. But the underground is not easy to use, so you should learn about it before you use it.

Writing home   Stamps can only be bought in post offices; but nearly every village (or part of a town) has a post office. Often it is inside a small shop.

Eating out   Restaurants are often expensive, and you cannot be sure the food will be good. But Indian and Chinese restaurants usually serve good meals at lower prices. Pubs sometimes do good inexpensive food. Fast food shops – fish and chip shops, hamburger shops – are cheap, but the food is not always very good.

Medical care   If you get ill or have an accident while you are in Britain, and you must be treated before you return home, you can get free medical care. Your country may have an agreement with Britain for other medical care, too; ask at the British embassy or consulate before you leave. You may need a special paper from your country's national health service. If your country does not have an agreement with Britain, you may want to take out health insurance for the journey.

2 Say these words after the teacher or the recording. Notice the difference in pronunciation between *sh* and *ch*.

1. should   shop   show
   British   wash   push
2. change   cheap   chip
   coach   teach   each

Now pronounce these words.

ship   shut   cheque   shower   cheers
switch   cash   fresh   watch   finish

3 Notice *can* in the text:

*. . . you **can** usually find at least one bank . . .*
*. . . tourist offices **can** help you to find these.*
*Stamps **can** only be bought in post offices; . . .*
*. . . you **cannot** be sure the food will be good.*
*. . . you **can** get free medical care.*

Now answer these questions.

1. What are seven things you can do in an airport?
   Example: *'You can have a meal.'*
2. What are five things you can and can't do in your city/town/village/neighbourhood?
   Examples: *'You can go swimming. You can't go skiing.'*

4 Look back at the text and decide whether *will* or *may* goes in each blank.

1. Not all banks in small towns in Britain .... change foreign money for you.
2. If you stay in a hotel in Britain, it .... be expensive.
3. Information centres .... have information about 'bed and breakfast'.
4. If 'bed and breakfast' is too expensive, there .... be a youth hostel nearby.
5. You .... have the choice between a train and a coach for travel from one city to another.
6. You .... only find stamps in post offices.
7. If you break your leg while on holiday in Britain, you .... not have to pay the hospital for treating it.

5 Look for these words in the text and notice how each one is used.

for example   but   these   also   it   and   so   too

Now choose one of the subjects from the opposite page (*Money, Where to stay*, etc.) and write about your own country or another country you know about. Try to use some of the words from the list. Then exchange papers with one or more students to read what they have written.

6 Listen.

1. Annie   Annie
2. Why?   Why?
3. in London   in London
4. July and August   July and August

Now listen again. Up ↗ or down ↘ ?

5. Annie
6. Why?
7. in London
8. July and August

7 Listen to the recording. Each time you hear a word or sentence, note whether it goes up ↗ or down ↘ at the end.

35

B Going to the USA

1 **What do you know about travelling in the USA? Try to answer these questions.**

1. A penny is worth one cent ($0.01, or 1¢). How much are these coins worth: a nickel, a dime, a quarter?
2. Can you usually find a bank in a small American town that will change foreign money?
3. In what places are you likely to find campsites in the US?
3. Is it easy to tour the United States by train?
5. What is the cheapest way of touring the States?

2 **Listen to the telephone conversation and write down the following information.**

1. the telephone numbers
2. the name of the person phoning
3. the time the plane will land
4. the airline and flight number

Now listen again and see if you can remember some of what was said.

3 **Work in threes. Imagine your wallet and passport have just been stolen in the airport in New York City. You were about to take a plane to Washington, and you still have your plane ticket and your traveller's cheques. Make some collect (reverse-charge) calls.**

1. To your friend Pat in Washington. Ask him/her to come and pick you up at the airport when you arrive. (Pat's phone number: (202) 664–3572)
2. To your cousin Chris, who lives in Newark, New Jersey, to ask him/her to phone and cancel your American Express and Diner's Club credit cards – you don't have the numbers of the cards, but your parents do. Chris can phone them if there is a problem. (Chris's number: (201) 435–2090)
3. To Mr/Ms Bennett, who is expecting you in Boston tomorrow. You will have to stay in Washington to go to your embassy and get a new passport. (The Bennetts' number: (617) 975–4303)

A

B

C

D

E

F

G

H

I

4 **Match the pictures and the phrases. Use your dictionary if you need to.**

1. a passport
2. light clothes
3. a pickpocket
4. customs
5. a visa
6. traveller's cheques
7. medical insurance
8. immigration control
9. sunglasses

5 Going to Miami. Make some sentences with *You'll have to ...* and *You should ...* for somebody who's going to Florida on holiday.

Examples: *'You should take sunglasses.'*
'You'll have to have a passport.'

> You should
> You'll have to

> have
> take
> watch out for
> go through
> buy

> a passport.
> light clothes.
> pickpockets.
> customs.
> a visa.

> traveller's cheques.
> medical insurance.
> immigration control.
> sunglasses.

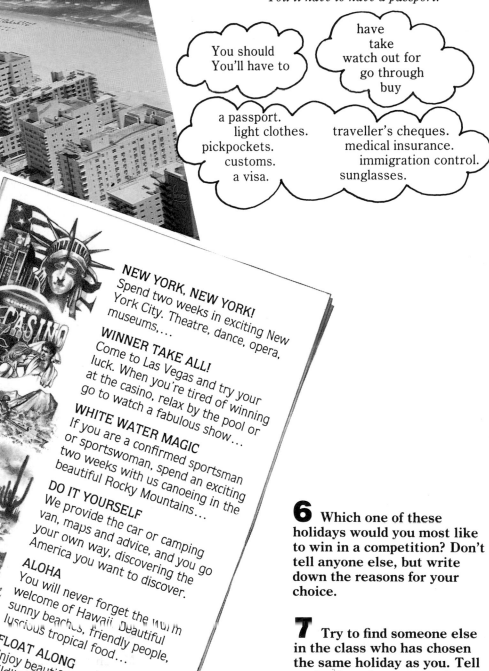

NEW YORK, NEW YORK!
Spend two weeks in exciting New York City. Theatre, dance, opera, museums,...

WINNER TAKE ALL!
Come to Las Vegas and try your luck. When you're tired of winning at the casino, relax by the pool or go to watch a fabulous show...

WHITE WATER MAGIC
If you are a confirmed sportsman or sportswoman, spend an exciting two weeks with us canoeing in the beautiful Rocky Mountains...

DO IT YOURSELF
We provide the car or camping van, maps and advice, and you go your own way, discovering the America you want to discover.

ALOHA
You will never forget the warm welcome of Hawaii. Beautiful sunny beaches, friendly people, luscious tropical food...

FLOAT ALONG
Enjoy beautiful Texas scenery and wildlife while relaxing on a raft on the Rio Grande. Comfortable tent accommodation at night...

6 Which one of these holidays would you most like to win in a competition? Don't tell anyone else, but write down the reasons for your choice.

7 Try to find someone else in the class who has chosen the same holiday as you. Tell each other the reasons for your choices.

Then find people who have chosen another holiday. Tell them what you think they will have to do and should do.

Problems

A Emergency

1 Match the pictures and the sentences.

1. My baby has just eaten some aspirins.
2. There's a fire in my kitchen.
3. There's been an accident. A man is hurt. He's bleeding badly.
4. There's been a burglary.
5. Smoke is coming out of my neighbour's kitchen window.
6. Somebody has stolen my motorbike.

2 The same or different? You will hear nine pairs of words. If the two words are the same, write 'S'. If they are different, write 'D'.

3 Can you hear a *th*? Copy the list; then listen and circle the words you hear.

1. then / den
2. there / dare
3. think / sink
4. thing / sing
5. those / doze

4 Practise saying these after your teacher or the recording.

There's a   There's a fire
There's a fire in my kitchen.

There's been
There's been an accident.
There's been a burglary.

through   put you through
I'll put you through.

there   right there
We'll be right there.

think   I think
I think his leg is broken.

5 Look at the pictures and report the emergencies. Your teacher will help you.
Example: 1. *'There's a fire in the bedroom.'*

6 Phoning about an emergency. Here are some instructions from a British phone box.

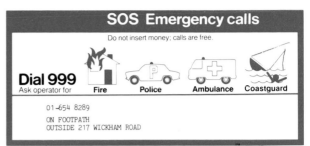

(Reproduced by permission of British Telecommunications.)

Now listen to the conversation and fill in the blanks.

OPERATOR: Emergency. .... service, ...?
FATHER: Ambulance.
OPERATOR: What .... are you ringing ....?
FATHER: ....
OPERATOR: Hold on. I'll .... you through.
OFFICER: .... Can I .... you?
FATHER: My .... has fallen off a ...., and I think his .... is broken.
OFFICER: Your .... and ...., please?
FATHER: Colin Jackson, ... Latton Close.
OFFICER: All right, ..., we'll be right there. .... cover your .... to keep him ...., but don't .... him.
FATHER: ....

7 Form groups of three. Choose emergencies from Exercises 1 and 5, or think of other emergencies. Invent and practise new conversations like the one in Exercise 6.

8 Think of an emergency in your life. Ask the teacher for any words you need to talk about it. Then tell the students around you what happened. Example:

'I wasn't very old, about 12. I was at home with my little brother. He pulled a very hot saucepan of soup on himself. I phoned...'

39

B You made me do it

1 Study and practise the dialogue. Your teacher will help you. Then work with a partner and make up a new dialogue, using some of the words and expressions you have learnt.

CRASH!

A: I'm sorry. I didn't mean to do it.
B: That's all right.
A: You see, I was thinking about something else. And I forgot what I was doing.
B: I see.
A: Actually, you made me do it.
B: I made you do it?
A: Yes. You coughed. You made me jump.
B: Yes. Well, it doesn't matter. We can get a new one.
A: I mean, it wasn't really my fault, was it?
B: No, it wasn't your fault.
A: I didn't do it on purpose.
B: No. Be careful!
A: It was an accident, you see.
B: Look out! Look out!!!
A: I mean, – **(CRASH!!!!!!!)**

2 Which picture? Listen to the sentences and write the answers. Example:

2. music

Then try to remember the sentence that goes with each picture.

| a light switch | a brake | music | hard work |
| an accelerator | rain | chocolate | a kiss |

3 Write four sentences of your own using *make*, like the ones in Exercise 2. Other students will try to guess what you have written about.

40

4 Read the story and put the pictures in order. Do not worry about the blanks.

A man had a row with his wife .... his breakfast was burnt. This made him leave home later than usual, ... he drove to work very fast. .... he was going round a corner, a dog ran across the road. The man stamped on the brakes, ... the car skidded (the road was in a very bad condition .... the City Council had not repaired it for a long time). The man lost control of his car .... crashed into a lorry .... was parked on a double yellow line.

Now put one of these words in each blank.

and	as	because	because	but
		so	which	

5 Write the story that goes with these pictures. Try to use some of the words from the box in Exercise 4.

6 How many words do you hear? (Contractions like *there's* count as two words.)

7 Listen to the song. How much can you understand? (Words on page 156.)

If and when

A If you see a black cat, …

1 Match the beginnings and the ends of these sentences.

If you are travelling at 80kph in a car,
If your ancestors' language was Choctaw,
If the score is 40–15,
If today is your golden wedding anniversary,
If your great-grandparents all had blue eyes,
If you travel from England to Scotland,
In the 18th century, if someone saw a dodo,
If last year was a leap year (with 366 days),
If you can speak French,

next year won't be a leap year.
they were on the island of Mauritius.
you have been married for 50 years.
you can understand at least a bit of Italian.
you have blue eyes.
you can stop safely in 52m.
you do not go through immigration control.
you are probably playing tennis.
they lived in America.

2 Superstitions. Do you believe in luck? Complete the sentences with words and expressions from the box.

1. If .... a black cat, you'll have good luck.
2. If .... some wine, ... some salt over your left shoulder to keep bad luck away.
3. If the sky .... this evening, the weather is going to be fine tomorrow.
4. If your first visitor in the New Year .... dark hair, ... good luck all year.
5. You'll have bad luck if you: .... under a ladder, ... an umbrella in the house, or .... a hat on a bed. If you .... a mirror, you'll have seven years' ....
6. If the palm of your .... hand itches, you're going to .... some money.

bad luck	break	get	has	is red
left	open	see	throw	walk
you'll have	you see	you spill		

3 Do you know any other superstitions?

4 What will happen if . . .?
Listen to the recording and
answer the questions.

5 *If* or *when*? Look at the difference.

When I go to bed tonight, I'll . . .
   (I *will* go to bed.)
If I go to Scotland, I'll . . .
   (I *may* go to Scotland.)

When you are on holiday, think of me.
   (You *will* be on holiday.)
If you are ever in London, come and see us.
   (You *may* be in London.)

1. .... I get rich, I'll travel round the world.
2. .... that's all you can say, I'm leaving.
3. .... I go to bed, I usually read for a few minutes.
4. .... you say that again, I'll hit you.
5. .... it rains this afternoon, we'll stay at home.
6. I'll close the curtains .... it gets dark.
7. .... I get older, I'll stop playing rugby.
8. Be patient; we can go home .... the game's finished.
9. Get on quickly .... the train stops.
10. .... you drive when you're drunk, you'll probably crash.

6 Listen to the recording
and do what the speaker tells
you.

7 Work in groups. Write
instructions like those in
Exercise 6 and give them to
another group.

8 Listen to the song once.
Then listen again and try to
remember the words that
have been left out.

43

B How to fill a kettle

1 Put a word or expression from the box into each blank. Then use the picture to help you put the sentences in order.

as soon as	then	then
until	when	when

.... it does this, it will turn the tap off.

When you do this, the cat will run, turning the tap on.

.... you want to fill the kettle, hook its handle to the string and turn the small wheel .... the kettle is under the tap.

.... lower the fish to the right side of the cat's wheel.

.... turn the small wheel again to get the kettle back.

.... the kettle is full, move the fish to the left side of the wheel, and the cat will run the other way.

2 Look at the pictures and say what will happen. Example:

1. 'When / As soon as she opens the door, the light will go on.'

44

3 Cooking tips. Put *when* or *until* in each blank.

1. Cook asparagus .... you can easily put a sharp knife through the middle of the stems.
2. If you need unsalted butter, pour boiling water over salted butter which has been cut into pieces, and then put it all into the fridge. .... the butter is hard, the salt will be left in the water.
3. .... you only need the yellow skin of a lemon, cut it with a potato peeler; this will cut it thinner than a knife.
4. If you are cooking whole onions, remember that they won't make you cry .... they lose their roots. So peel them from the top and cut the roots off last.
5. Serve vodka very cold. Keep it on ice .... the moment you pour it.
6. .... a melon is ready to eat, the end opposite the stem will be fairly soft.

(from *Supertips* by Moyra Bremner – adapted)

4 Work in groups. Make a list of three or more cooking tips to tell the class.

5 How do you tell when a cake or a loaf of bread is done? Listen, and complete the sentences.

1. Stick a needle in and see if...
2. Press it on the top and if it springs up again, ...
3. Tap...
4. Cut...
5. Listen to it to see...
6. See if it's shrunk...

Now match the numbered sentences to the pictures.

6 Pronunciation. Pronounce these words.

1. handle cat back tap
2. way make cake
3. sharp hard class last
4. small all
5. want water what

You probably don't know these words. How do you think they are pronounced?

bark failing crack delayed
craft angle harm flash swab
tray wand sprain paw rate
stall nap vast balk shaft

7 In groups, invent a way of doing one of these things. Describe your invention to the other groups; you can draw pictures if you want.

1. Putting your shoes on without bending down
2. Opening and closing a window
3. Picking apples
4. Cleaning high windows
5. Washing socks

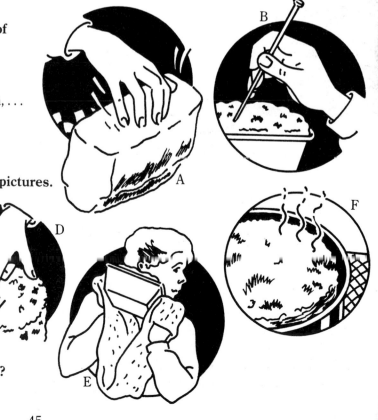

Now can you guess what these words mean?

needle spring tap bubble shrink

Revision and fluency practice

A A choice of activities

> Look at the exercises in this lesson. Try to decide which of them are most useful for you, and do three or more.

GRAMMAR REVISION

1 Choose the correct tense (present or present perfect).

1. How long *do you know / have you known* Mary?
2. *I live / I've lived* here for eight years.
3. *I'm going / I've been* home on Sunday.
4. *I have / I've had* this car since 1982.
5. Sorry I'm late. *Are you waiting / Have you been waiting* long?

2 Choose the correct tense (present perfect or simple past).

1. *Have you ever seen / Did you ever see* a boxing match?
2. *Have you ever been / Did you ever go* camping when you were a child?
3. Where *have you had / did you have* lunch yesterday?
4. Where's the telephone? *There's been / There was* an accident!
5. *I've never travelled / I never travelled* by air.
6. Can you help me? *I've lost / I lost* my watch.
7. *I've lost / I lost* my glasses the other day.
8. '*Have you had / 'Did you have* breakfast?' 'Not yet.'

3 Choose the correct tense (simple or progressive).

1. 'Could I speak to Linda?' 'I'm afraid *she puts / she's putting* the baby to bed. Could you ring back in about half an hour?'
2. I first met my wife when I *worked / was working* in Detroit.
3. How often *do you see / are you seeing* your parents?
4. My father *worked / was working* in Nigeria for a long time when he was younger.
5. *Do you know / Are you knowing* my friend Alex Carter?
6. 'Would you like a cigarette?' 'No, thanks, *I don't smoke / I'm not smoking.*'
7. 'What *do you do / are you doing*?' '*I try / 'I'm trying* to mend my bicycle. Would you like to help?'
8. 'What *do you do / are you doing*?' 'I'm a chemical engineer.'
9. 'I called at your house yesterday evening, but you weren't there. What *did you do / were you doing*?' 'I was at a party.'
10. 'What *did you do / were you doing* after the party?' 'I went straight home.'

LISTENING

4 Listen to the news broadcast and answer the questions.

1. The Distillers' Company are planning to 'axe' some jobs. How many – more than a hundred or less than a hundred? And how many plants are they going to close?
2. Three youths attacked a nineteen-year-old airman. Did he have to go to hospital? Was any money stolen, and if so, how much?
3. Two women tried to use a stolen credit card. What did they try to buy?   a) wine   b) spirits c) cigarettes   d) a car.
   What colour car did they drive away in? Can you describe them at all?
4. People in Amport go to church for an unusual reason. What is it?
5. What has been stolen in Cassington, near Witney?   a) camping equipment   b) cooking equipment   c) a camera from a kitchen d) camera attachments.
6. Which of these words do you hear in the weather forecast?
   cool   cold   clouds   cloudy   snow showers   sunny intervals   wet   dry nineteen   ninety   north-westerly north-easterly   winds   strong   Tuesday

5 Listen to the conversation. Every time you hear the name of a food, write 'F'; every time you hear the name of a drink, write 'D'.
Listen a second time. Write down an example of each of these: a hard thing, a soft thing, a liquid, a solid, a countable noun, an uncountable noun.

6 Pronunciation. Listen to the conversation. How many times do you hear *there's* and *there are* ? Make a note each time.

READING AND WRITING

7 Are you a peaceful person? Answer the questions as honestly as you can and then find out your total score. (But don't take the test too seriously!)

1. If you have ever been in a political demonstration, score 2.
2. If you have lost your temper during the last three days, score 3.
3. If you have ever driven at over 160kph, score 2.
4. If you have ever broken a cup, glass or plate on purpose, score 1.
5. If you have been in a fight in the last three years, score 3.
6. If you have seen a war film, gangster film, western or other violent film in the last month, score 1.
7. If you have ever been in love with two people at the same time, score 2.
8. If you ever have violent dreams, score 1.
9. If you have ever walked out of a job, score 2.
10. If you have ever watched a boxing-match, score 2.
11. If you like the town better than the country, score 1.

Your score:

0–7:   You are a very peaceful person.
8–13:   Average.
14–20:   You are not at all peaceful!

8 Now make up your own questionnaire.
Suggestions: find out whether people are energetic, polite, cultured, generous, honest, shy, careful with money, fashion-conscious, interested in sport, interested in politics, sociable.

SPEAKING

9 'What's my job?' Choose a job and mime it (act it without speaking) to the other students. They will say what they think you are.

10 'What am I playing?' Choose a game or a musical instrument. Mime it to the other students. They will say what you are playing.

11 'What are we talking about?' Work in groups of three. Prepare a conversation in which somebody asks for something, or asks somebody else to do something. When you are ready, mime your conversation (without using the words) for the other students. They will try to find the words.

Are you a painter?
You're a conductor.
I think he's a policeman.
You're playing the harp.
Are you playing cricket?
Perhaps she's playing tennis.

12 Descriptions: revision. Read the conversation. Then work with a partner and make up a similar conversation about something that has been lost. Try to use the words and expressions in italics.

A: *I've lost* a briefcase.
B: Oh, yes? *What's it like?* Can you describe it?
A: It's brown, *with* a handle on top, and *it's got* a brass lock. It's about this big.
B: Anything inside it?
A: Yes. *There are* some books *with* my name *in,* and there's a pen *that* I bought yesterday. And a pint of milk.
B: *Where did you lose it?*
A: I think *I left it* on the number 14 bus.
B: Well, *I'll see what I can do.*

13 Question-box. Each student writes three questions on separate pieces of paper. One of the questions must begin *Have you ever...?*, and one must begin *Do you...?* The questions are folded up and put in a box. Students take turns to draw out questions and answer them.

47

B Knife-thrower's assistant wanted

WELL-KNOWN NORTHERN MANUFACTURER
requires
SALES MANAGER
for district between Liverpool and Carlisle.
Very good .....1...... and conditions.
Use of new company car.
.....2..... between 25 and 40.
Previous selling .....3..... essential.
.....4..... to: Managing Director, Domestic
Engineering Services Ltd, 417 North Way,
Whitehaven, Cumbria WN6 4DJ.

---

1 Read the advertisement and the two letters. Fill in the numbered gaps with words and expressions from the box. (You can use a dictionary, or ask your teacher about difficult words.)

advertised	age	apply	companies
engineering	experience	faithfully	
look forward	salary	Sales Manager	
several	should like	worked	write

---

17 Grove Crescent
Greendale
Cumbria CU6 7LY

May 24, 1985

The Managing Director
Domestic Engineering Services Ltd
417 North Way
Whitehaven
Cumbria WN6 4DJ

Dear Sir

I ..5... to apply for the post of ...6... advertised
in the Guardian of 22 May. I am 36 years old and
have experience of selling in ...7.... firms.
I also have qualifications in ..8...

I look forward to hearing from you.

Yours faithfully

Roger Parsons

---

35 Allendale Road,
Carlisle
CA2 4SJ.

23 May, 1985

Dear Sir,
I wish to ...9.... for the job of Sales
Manager ...10... in yesterday's Guardian.
I have a Higher National Diploma in
Business Studies, and have ...11.... as a
Sales Manager for two large ...12.... I am 29.
I ...13.... to hearing from you.

Yours ...14...,

Andrew Jardine

---

2 Here are some sentences from four letters from Domestic Engineering Services Ltd to Mr Parsons and Mr Jardine. (The sentences are not in order; some of them come in more than one letter.) Can you write one of the letters?

Dear Mr ......
Yours sincerely
Please come for an interview on .... at .... a.m.
Thank you for your letter of .... May.
Please confirm your acceptance as soon as
    possible.
Thank you for coming for an interview yesterday.
We regret that we are unable to offer you the
    post.
We are pleased to offer you the position of
    Sales Manager, starting on 1 August, at a
    salary of £12,500 a year.

---

3 Read the advertisements with a dictionary.

ROSTON TIMES

MANAGER FOR SMALL NEWSAGENTS

Applicants must have experience
of running a small shop.
Good knowledge of accounting desirable.
Aged 25–40.
Apply in writing to:
Personnel Manager
Chambers and Wren
Chambers House
High Street
Barbury BA6 10S.

Efficient
SHORTHAND TYPIST/SECRETARY
needed for small friendly company.
Apply to Office Manageress, Ann Harper Ltd,
6 Newport Road, Roston RS1 4JX.

FULL-TIME GARDENER
wanted for Roston General Hospital.
Experience essential.
Good wages and conditions.
Apply: The Administrator.

TEACHER REQUIRED
for private language school.
Teaching experience unnecessary.
Apply: The Director of Studies
Instant Languages Ltd
279 Canal Street, Roston.

CLEANER
required for our Roston office,
hours by arrangement. Apply The
Manager Coleman and Stokes 33
South Parade Roston RS1 5BQ.

Full-time
DRIVERS
required
Clean driving licence
Must be of smart appearance
Aged over 25.
Apply
CAPES TAXIS
17 Palace Road
Roston.

SECRETARY
(good Audio/Shorthand)

CABIN STAFF
Southern Airlines require cabin staff for
intercontinental flights. Applicants must be
between 20 and 33 years old, height 1m60 to
1m75, education to GCE standard, two
languages, must be able to swim. Apply to
Recruitment Officer, Southern Airlines,
Heathrow Airport West, HR3 7KK.

PART-TIME JOB
Circus has an unexpected vacancy for a
knife-thrower's assistant. Excellent pay. Apply in
writing to City Show Office, 13 Rose Lane, Roston.

SECRETARIES

SECRETA ASSISTA

PA/SECRE

---

4 Job interviews. Work in groups of about
six (three interviewers and three applicants).
1. Applicants write letters of application for
   one of the jobs advertised; interviewers
   prepare interviews.
2. Applicants are interviewed in turn.
3. Interviewers choose the best applicant and
   write letters to all three.

Where do you work? How long have you been there?
Why do you want to change your job? Where did
you go to school? Have you any experience of
selling? Can you speak any foreign languages?
Have you ever lived abroad? Have you ever been
dismissed from a job? What are your interests?
Are you married?

What's the salary? What are the hours?

Causes and origins

Paper-making centuries ago

Wood fibres magnified

A From tree to paper

1 Read the text with a dictionary, and put one of these words into each blank: *paper, wood, trees.* Ask the teacher for help if necessary.

> Excuse me. What does 'invented' mean?

> Excuse me. I don't understand this.

> Excuse me. Can you explain this word?

> Excuse me. How do you pronounce this?

......1...... was invented by the Chinese in the first century AD. The art of ......2......-making took 700 years to reach the Muslim world and another 700 years to get to Britain (via Spain, southern France and Germany).

Most ......3...... is made from ......4....... When ......5...... are cut down, they are transported by land or water to paper mills. Here they are cut up and the ......6...... is broken up into fibres, which are mixed with water and chemicals. This ......7...... pulp is then dried on a machine and made into ......8.......

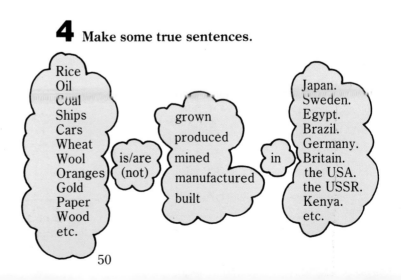

Paper-making today

Future paper

......9......-making is an important British industry, and ......10...... from Britain is exported to South Africa, Australia and many other countries. Some of the ......11...... used in the British paper-making industry comes from ......12...... grown in Britain, but ......13...... is also imported from other countries such as Norway. One tree is needed for every 400 copies of a typical forty-page newspaper. If half the adults in Britain each buy one daily ......14......, this uses up over 40,000 ......15...... a day. ......16...... are being cut down faster than they are being replaced, so there may be a serious paper shortage before the year 2000.

2 Close your book and listen to the sentences. Are they true or false?

3 The word *America* (/əˈmerɪkə/) has the sound /ə/ twice. Which ten of the following words also contain the sound /ə/?

iron century paper
correct Germany adults
fibre replaced pulp
machine industry exported
Africa countries Norway
needed serious shortage

4 Make some true sentences.

| Rice Oil Coal Ships Cars Wheat Wool Oranges Gold Paper Wood etc. | is/are (not) | grown produced mined manufactured built | in | Japan. Sweden. Egypt. Brazil. Germany. Britain. the USA. the USSR. Kenya. etc. |

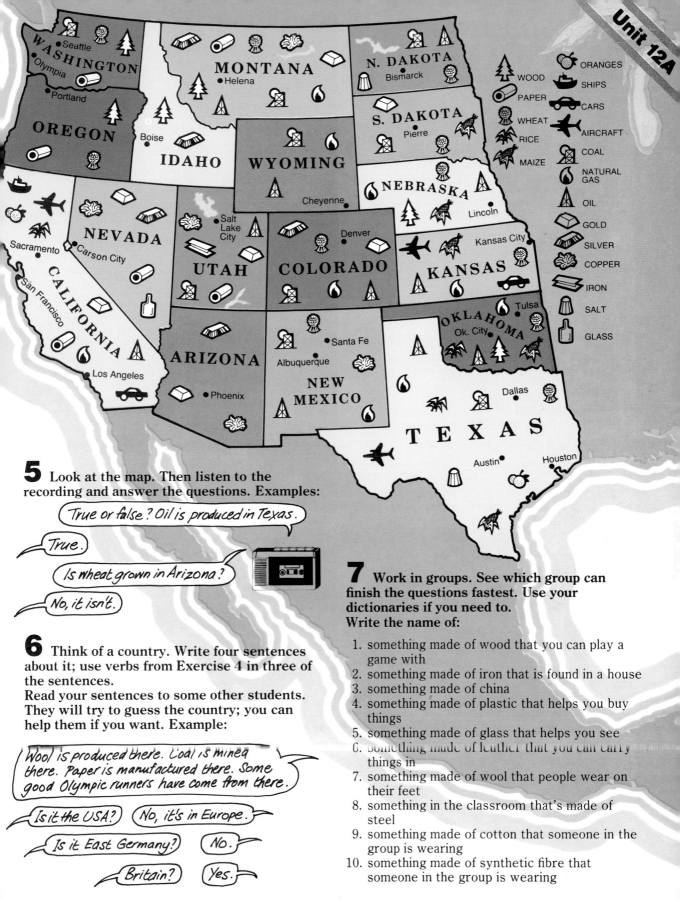

5 Look at the map. Then listen to the recording and answer the questions. Examples:

True or false? Oil is produced in Texas.

True.

Is wheat grown in Arizona?

No, it isn't.

6 Think of a country. Write four sentences about it; use verbs from Exercise 4 in three of the sentences.
Read your sentences to some other students. They will try to guess the country; you can help them if you want. Example:

Wool is produced there. Coal is mined there. Paper is manufactured there. Some good Olympic runners have come from there.

Is it the USA? *No, it's in Europe.*

Is it East Germany? *No.*

Britain? *Yes.*

7 Work in groups. See which group can finish the questions fastest. Use your dictionaries if you need to.
Write the name of:

1. something made of wood that you can play a game with
2. something made of iron that is found in a house
3. something made of china
4. something made of plastic that helps you buy things
5. something made of glass that helps you see
6. something made of leather that you can carry things in
7. something made of wool that people wear on their feet
8. something in the classroom that's made of steel
9. something made of cotton that someone in the group is wearing
10. something made of synthetic fibre that someone in the group is wearing

51

B Who killed Harrison?

1 Grammar. Look at the examples. Then write the infinitives and past participles of the verbs below.

INFINITIVE:	Can you **make** an omelette?
	I want **to see** the manager.
	We need **to import** less.
PAST TENSE:	She **made** that dress herself.
	I **saw** Alan yesterday.
	We **imported** 4m tons last year.
PAST PARTICIPLE	I've **made** you a cake.
	I haven't **seen** her today.
	We have **imported** more this year.
	Paper is **made** from wood.
	He was last **seen** in Cairo.
	This was **imported** from Taiwan.

1. know   steal   go   drink
2. find   build   think
3. mix   question   kill   arrest   need   export
4. manufacture   use   dry

2 Put the *-ing* form or the past participle.

1. 'What are you doing?' 'I'm .... bread.' (*make*)
2. Paper is .... from wood. (*make*)
3. When was that church ....?(*build*)
4. Mary and John are .... their own house. (*build*)
5. Why are you .... up that chair? (*break*)
6. I think the window was .... by a stone. (*break*)
7. Too many trees are .... down every year. (*cut*)
8. When we arrived, she was .... his hair. (*cut*)
9. The police are .... him now. (*question*)
10. When she was ...., she said nothing. (*question*)

7 Read the following text, but do *not* look at the text on the opposite page. Then work with a partner, and ask him or her questions to get more complete information about Harrison's death.

HARRISON was last seen alive at 9.30 p.m. (*Where?*) He was found dead in his flat by his wife Mary when she came home from a dance. (*What time?*) He was killed with a revolver. A small French-English dictionary was found by his body. (*Anything else? Was anything stolen?*)

The police suspect Haynes, MacHale and Cannon. All three were arrested the next morning.

HAYNES once worked for Harrison, but was sacked. (*Why?*) He has often said he hates Harrison, and would like to kill him. He was seen by three witnesses at 10.30. (*Where?*) When he was arrested, a revolver was found in his car. (*Where were his fingerprints found?*)

MacHALE is known to the police as a thief, but not as a killer. (*Where is he from?*) He is an old friend of Harrison's. (*Does he know Mrs Harrison?*) When he was arrested, £2,000 in cash was found in his wallet. (*Anything else?*)

CANNON works in an import-export business. (*Where?*) Harrison owed him a lot of money. When he was questioned, he said that he was at his hotel from 9.30 to 11.30. (*What did his wife say?*) He was seen earlier coming out of Harrison's flat. (*What time?*) Cannon's wife is an old friend of Mary Harrison's.

WHO DO YOU THINK KILLED HARRISON?

3 Make some true sentences.

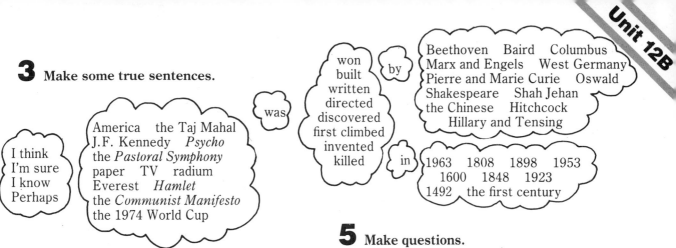

I think
I'm sure
I know
Perhaps

America   the Taj Mahal
J.F. Kennedy   *Psycho*
the *Pastoral Symphony*
paper   TV   radium
Everest   *Hamlet*
the *Communist Manifesto*
the 1974 World Cup

was

won
built
written
directed
discovered
first climbed
invented
killed

by

Beethoven   Baird   Columbus
Marx and Engels   West Germany
Pierre and Marie Curie   Oswald
Shakespeare   Shah Jehan
the Chinese   Hitchcock
Hillary and Tensing

in

1963   1808   1898   1953
1600   1848   1923
1492   the first century

Now listen to the recording.

4 Who, what, when, where, why, how? Listen to the answers and write the question-words. Examples:

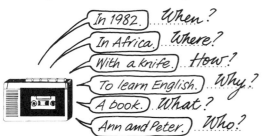

In 1982.   *When?*
In Africa.   *Where?*
With a knife.   *How?*
To learn English.   *Why?*
A book.   *What?*
Ann and Peter.   *Who?*

5 Make questions.

1. Gloria gets up very early. (*'What time...?'*)
2. The church was built by Wren. (*'When...?'*)
3. I'm waiting. (*'What...?'*)
4. He was sacked last week. (*'Why...?'*)
5. We're going on holiday in July. (*'Where...?'*)
6. I don't usually sit here. (*'Where...?'*)
7. He never travels by car. (*'How...?'*)
8. My father was killed when I was six. (*'How...?'*)

6 Pronunciation. Pronounce these words.

here   half   home   Harrison   hated   who
hand   hungry   happy

Listen and write what you hear.

7 Read the following text, but do *not* look at the text on the opposite page. Then work with a partner, and ask him or her questions to get more complete information about Harrison's death.

HARRISON was last seen alive talking to a woman in the street outside his flat in central London. (*What time?*) He was found dead by his wife (*Name?*) when she came home from a dance at 11.30. (*How was he killed?*) A Paris underground ticket was found by his body. (*Anything else?*) His wallet had been stolen.

The police suspect Haynes, MacHale and Cannon. All three were arrested the next morning.

HAYNES once worked for Harrison, but was sacked for stealing. He has often said he hates Harrison, and would like to kill him. He was seen by three witnesses 50km from Harrison's home. (*What time?*) His fingerprints were found in Harrison's flat. When he was arrested, his car was searched by the police. (*Was anything found?*)

MacHALE is from Scotland. He is a very old friend of Mrs Harrison's. (*Did he know Mr Harrison?*) When he was arrested, a love letter (signed '*Mary*') was found in his pocket. (*Anything else? Find out if MacHale is known to the police.*)

CANNON works in Paris. (*What does he do? Find out if he owed Harrison money.*) He was seen coming out of Harrison's flat at 9.15. When his wife was questioned, she said that he was out of his hotel all evening. (*What did he say? Find out if Cannon's wife knows Mary Harrison.*)

WHO DO YOU THINK KILLED HARRISON?

Descriptions

A Places

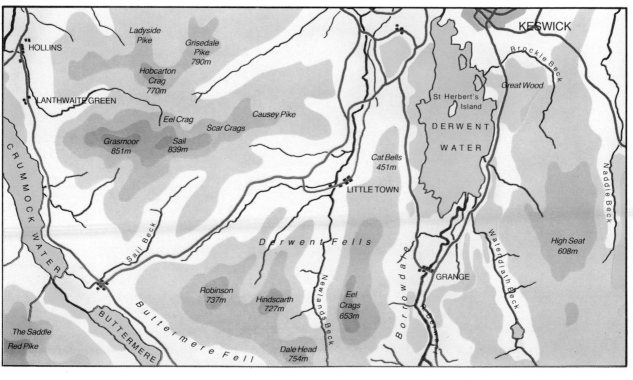

1 Look at the picture. Which word goes with which number?

hill   mountain   valley   wood   stream
waterfall   island   river   lake   bridge
path   road

2 How do you get from A to B? Use the words in Exercise 1 with these prepositions.

across   through   along   up   down

Example: *'You go down the hill, . . .'*

3 Look at the map and listen to the recording. Decide whether the sentences are true or false. Example:

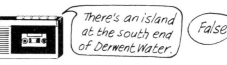

There's an island at the south end of Derwent Water.

False.

4 Pronunciation. Listen to the recording. How many words do you hear in each sentence? What are they? (Contractions like *there's* count as two words.)

5 Look at the town plan. Imagine that somebody asked you how to get from the car park to the post office. What would you say? If you don't know the answer, put these sentences in order.

Then take the first left.
You'll see it on your left.
Then turn right at the first crossroads.
Go straight ahead for about 200 metres.
Keep straight on past the station.

6 Work in groups. Ask and give directions from the car park to other places on the map. Example:

'Excuse me. Can you tell me the way to the Rainbow Theatre?'
'Yes. Go straight ahead ...'

7 Can you write down the names of all the rooms in a typical house?

8 Read the advertisement and listen to the recording. How many differences can you find between the two descriptions of the house?

Central York
MAGNIFICENT TOWN RESIDENCE

Four double bedrooms, luxury bathroom, upstairs and downstairs cloakrooms, lounge, dining-room, kitchen/breakfast room, double garage, beautiful mature garden, gas-fired central heating. In first-class condition.

£90,000

9 Work in groups of three or four. Tell the other students in the group about a place that you like. It can be somewhere in the country, a town, a street, a building, or any other kind of place.

10 Listen to the song, and see how much you can understand. Then look at the words on page 156, listen again, and sing along.

B Things

1 Listen to the conversation and learn the new words and expressions.

A: Funny, isn't it?
B: Yes. I didn't think it would be so big.
A: No.
B: Do you like it?
A: I don't know. I'm not sure. Give me time.
B: It looks heavy.
A: Yes, it's quite heavy. Try and pick it up.
B: Ooooh! My back!
A: See?
B: It feels really cold. Like ice.
A: I know.
B: And it smells funny.
A: Sort of sweet.
B: Yes. What's that thing on the top? What's it for?
A: I don't know. Perhaps it's to open the lid with.
B: Fred.
A: Yes, Pete?
B: What *is* it?

2 Put these words and expressions into the sentences.

a bit	feel	funny	isn't it	like	looks
smells	so	sort of	sure	think	with

1. 'Is that Mary?' 'I'm not ....'
2. 'Do you like my hair like this?' 'Not really. I think it looks a bit ....'
3. It was a good film. But I didn't .... it would be .... long.
4. Your sister looks .... you.
5. My brother looks .... like my father.
6. 'The house .... funny.' 'Yes, I've been cooking fish.'
7. I .... funny. ...., hot and cold all over.
8. It's cold today, ... ?
9. That baby .... like a football .... arms and legs.

3 Listen to the recording and say what you think the things might be. Begin *It sounds like...* Example:

'It sounds like a train.'

4 What are these?

1. A thing that takes you from place to place.
2. A thing that tells you the time.
3. A thing (that) you read to find out what has happened in the world.
4. A thing (that) you sit on.
5. A thing (that) you open the door with.
6. A thing (that) you drink out of.
7. A small animal with long ears.
8. An animal that has a very long neck.
9. An animal that has black and white stripes.
10. A very big animal with a very long nose.

In sentences 3–6, the word *that* can be left out. In sentences 1 and 2, it can't. Why?

5 How quickly can you match the words and the descriptions?

boat	calendar	envelope	gun	hairbrush
ice-cream	microphone	pillow	suitcase	
tap	tongue	wrist		

1. A thing water comes out of.
2. A thing you tidy your hair with.
3. Something that makes you cool in hot weather.
4. Something you put a letter in.
5. A part of your body that joins your hand to your arm.
6. A thing you can travel in across water.
7. Something you put your head on at night.
8. A thing you speak into.
9. A thing that can kill people.
10. Something that tells you the date.
11. A thing that is useful when you travel.
12. Something you use for talking and tasting.

6 Now describe these.

a church

a nail

a pig

a rose

a magazine

a suit

a sheet

a sandwich

an umbrella

a lipstick

an overcoat

Make up descriptions of some more things. See if the other students can work out what they are.

7 Pronunciation. Say these words and expressions.

1. is   it   didn't   think   big   thing   with   lid
   pick   liquid
2. It feels cold.   Eat it.   What is it?
   Is it liquid?
3. like   time   quite   alive   white   mine
4. light   high   tight   might   right   flight
5. give   pint   bicycle   litre

9 Twenty questions. One student thinks of something. The student doesn't tell the others what it is; he/she only tells them that it is 'animal', 'vegetable', 'mineral' or 'abstract'. (For example: a leather handbag is animal, a newspaper is vegetable, a glass is mineral and an idea is abstract.) The other students must find out what the thing is by asking questions (maximum 20); the only answers allowed are *Yes* and *No*. Useful questions:

Can you eat it?
Is it made of wood/metal/glass?
Is it useful?
Can you find it in a house/shop/car?
Is it liquid?
Is it hard/soft/heavy/light?
Have you got one of these?
Is there one in this room? In this building?
Is it manufactured?

8 Match the numbers and the pictures.

	LIQUID OR SOLID?	ALIVE?	USEFUL?	CAN YOU EAT/ DRINK IT?	MANUFAC- TURED?	CAN YOU WEAR IT?
1	S	NO	YES	YES	NO	NO
2	L	NO	YES	YES	YES	NO
3	S	YES	YES	NO	NO	NO
4	S	NO	YES	NO	YES	YES
5	S	NO	YES	NO	YES	NO
6	L	NO	YES	NO	YES	NO
7	S	NO	NO	NO	NO	YES

10 Listen to the recording of some people playing 'Twenty questions'.

a sweater

a pint of beer

a pearl

a litre of oil

a bicycle

a cat

a boiled egg

57

Families

A Different kinds of families

1 Match the texts and the pictures. You can use a dictionary.

1. Don and Lola are Kenny's grandparents. Kenny has lived with them since he was a baby. Last year they adopted him as their own child.
2. Kim and May are married, but they do not want to have children. Although they enjoy playing with their nieces and nephews, they do not want to be full-time parents.
3. John and Christine have got three children – Simon, Lucy and Emma. There are a lot of couples with young children in their neighbourhood, so they often help one another out.
4. Anamita has got four children. Besides her husband, Surendra, and the children, she also shares her home with her mother-in-law, her brother-in-law and his wife. The children get on well with their aunt and uncle, and like listening to their grandmother's stories.
5. Claire and Bridget live together. They both work outside the home and share the care of Beth, Bridget's six-year-old daughter.
6. Ann has been divorced for ten years. Her two children, Jason and Ruth, live with Ann, and see their father almost every week.
7. Because Jack is too ill to live alone, he lives with his son Barry, who is 25. Barry is getting married soon, and Jack will continue to live with the young couple. He hopes to have grandchildren to look after soon.

2 Pronouncing words together. Some words change their pronunciation before vowels. Listen to the differences in pronunciation.

1. they   they adopted him
2. who   who is 25
3. Claire   Claire and Bridget

Now pronounce these.

4. she also shares
5. too ill to live alone
6. their aunt and uncle
7. Barry is getting married
8. see their father almost every week
9. the care of Beth

3 How many words do you know for talking about relatives? Make a list beginning *mother, father,...* and see how many words you can add.

4 Tell other students about your family or other families you know. Examples:

'My uncle is divorced. His son...'
'My neighbours have got six children. ...'

58

5 Find these words in the texts in Exercise 1.

| also although and because |
| besides but so |

Now put one of the words into each blank in this text.

.... there are many different kinds of families in the world, there are some things that are the same everywhere. Not all societies have western-type marriage with one wife and one husband, ... some kind of marriage is universal. And when a person marries, ... the new wife or husband, he or she also gets a complete new family of in-laws. Marriages with close relatives do not always produce healthy children, ... all societies have rules about who can marry who. Each society .... has a division of work based on age and sex. In modern western societies, there is a move to change this last rule .... it can be unfair to women, ... it will be interesting to see if this succeeds.

6 Class survey. Make sure you understand the questions. Then choose one question to ask the other people in the class.

a. Would you like to live alone part of the time – say, one week a month?
b. Would you rather have more or fewer brothers and sisters than you have?
c. Would you like to have children? How many? OR: Would you like to have more or fewer children than you have?
d. Would you rather live in the same town as your parents or not?
e. Would you rather spend less time working and more time with your family?
f. Would you rather give your parents the money to have a nice holiday on their own, or take them on holiday with you?
g. Would you rather invite your in-laws to spend a week with you, or stay at home while your husband/wife visits them?
h. What's the best age for having children? Is it better to be young or a bit older?

7 Report the results of your survey. Example:

'Nine people would rather spend less time working and more time with their families, and six people think they see enough of their families.'

8 Listen to the recording. Some British people are answering questions from the survey. As you hear their answers, write the letters of the questions they are answering.

9 Listen to the song and try to write down the verbs.

MY OLD DAD

We never .... him in the mornings
And he always .... home late
Then he .... and .... the paper
And .... the crossword while he ....

He never .... us with our homework
But he .... me how to swim
And he .... me to be patient
I guess I .... a lot from him

My old dad
He was one of the good guys
He was nobody's hero
But he was special to me

Every summer we .... to Blackpool
Except when he .... unemployed
He .... to .... and .... the sunset
That .... one thing we both ....

He .... always very gentle
Nothing ever .... him mad
He .... never rich or famous
But I .... proud of my old dad

My old dad
He was one of the good guys
He was nobody's hero
But he was special to me

10 Tell other students about someone in your family that you are proud of.

59

B Family life

Dear God,
Are boys better
than girls, I
Know you are one
but try to be
fair.

Sylvia.

My mother said she
won't get maried again
it's too much truble

my mum only likes
little babies. when they
get old Like me She
smacks them.

If they don't want
You to make
your own break-
fast they
Should say
So before

Timmy

1 **Listen to the conversation.
Can you fill in the missing words?**

MIKE: Do you think housewives .... be .... in the same
.... as other people ....? I mean, everybody
.... who does a regular job .... a salary.

SUE: Yeah, but who .... them? That's the trouble. I mean, who
.... they be paid by? The only way you could do it is by
.... the man enough of a wage to pay you as well. And
that, that, er, I mean, in our .... age, in my parents' age
anyway, my .... was paid ...., um, to pay, to support
his wife and .... Nowadays that's not always ....

JOHN: There's no, there's no way you could pay a .... now.
She's doing about ten jobs.

2 **Listen to the conversation. You will hear
four of the expressions listed below. Which
ones?**

the wife stays at home   comes home to work
the end of his day's work
the end of the wife's working day
to work until midnight   If you both share
Well, that's it   I'll pick my feet up
I'll read the newspaper

3 One, two or three stresses? Put the expressions from the box into three lists. Example:

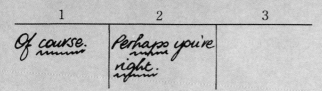

1	2	3
Of course.	Perhaps you're right.	

Of course. Perhaps. Yes, I think so.
No, I don't agree. I'm not sure. I agree.
Well, it depends. Probably. Yes, and...
No, I don't think so. Yes, definitely.
Of course not. Oh, I don't know.
Yes, but... Right. Perhaps you're right.

Now put the expressions in order, going from strong agreement to strong disagreement.

4 Work in groups. Each student should choose one of the sentences below, and make sure that all the other group members say what they think about it.

1. Housewives should be paid a salary.
2. Husbands should do some of the housework.
3. Children should do some of the housework.
4. Even young children should get regular pocket money.
5. Children should be free to choose their own friends.
6. When children are 16, they should be free to do what they like.

5 Write a sentence yourself about family life. See if other students agree with it.

6 Turn to the page your teacher tells you. Invent the other half of the dialogue. Write *only* the invented half on a sheet of paper. Then close your book and find a partner to make a complete dialogue with.

mothers and other nasty people frighten children to make them be good

Women do the washing up and cleaning and cooking and men go on the train and get tired.

You should never hit a baby because it can't hit back

Hopes and wishes

A Would you like to have a white Rolls Royce?

1 Listen to the recording and write down a phrase from the box for each blank.

> I'd like to   I'd like to   I'd like to
> I'd really like to   I'd really like
> I would like to   I *would* like
> I'd love to   I'd just like to

KEITH: .... work in a museum.
JOHN: I think .... own me own gardening centre. I'd love that. (*Yeah*) Yeah. .... that.
SUE: .... be a really good potter. (*Hm-hm. Yeah.*) Be on my own. (*Yeah*)
JANE: .... be really good at something.
ALEX: Actually with the job I've chosen, the police force, ... go into dog handling in that. That's what ....
KATY: I think .... teach again.
MIKE: What .... spend my time doing isn't really classed as jobs.

2 Work in groups. Make some true sentences.

> I'd /I would
> My sister would
> My husband would
> etc.

> (really)

> like to
> love to

> work...
> own...
> be a really good...
> be really good at...
> go into...
> ... again.
> spend my time...

Now close your books and tell some people from other groups what was said in your group. Examples:

'*Michiko would like to go into accounting.*'
'*Kurt's sister would love to own a horse.*'

3 Pronunciation. Listen to the words, and try to pronounce them correctly.

no so go hope know broke spoke over don't won't
open closed Rome phone

Now listen to the definitions, and say which words the speaker is talking about.

Example:

The past of 'speak'. *Spoke.*

4 Look at the questions and prepare your answers. You can answer as follows:

> '*Yes.*' '*I think so.*' '*I don't think so.*'
> '*I hope so.*' '*I hope not.*' '*I don't know.*'
> '*No.*' '*No, I don't.*' '*No, I won't.*'

When you are ready, close your book, listen to the questions, and answer them.

1. Will you live to be 100 years old?
2. Will you get married next year?
3. Is it going to rain tomorrow?
4. Will everyone come to the next English class?
5. Will you be ill next week?
6. Are there going to be any Olympic Games in the year 2000?
7. Do you hope to travel to America some day?
8. Do you dream in English?
9. What did your teacher want to do when he/she was younger?
10. Will you be very rich one day?
11. Did anyone in your class want to be a doctor when they were younger?
12. Would you like to go to the moon?

5 What did you want to be or do when you were younger? Write three sentences and give them to the teacher. Then try to guess whose sentences the teacher is reading.

> I wanted to be...
> I wanted to study...
> I wanted to...

> but
> and

> my parents wanted me to...
> my teachers wanted me to...
> I changed my mind.
> I still want...
> now I...

6 Choose another member of the class. Write a letter.

> Dear ....,
> I think you *want to / are going to / hope to / are going to try to* .... *by 1995 / by the end of the year / before you are 80* etc.; and I think
> .... Am I right?
> Yours,
> ....

Now answer the letter(s) you have received.
Example:

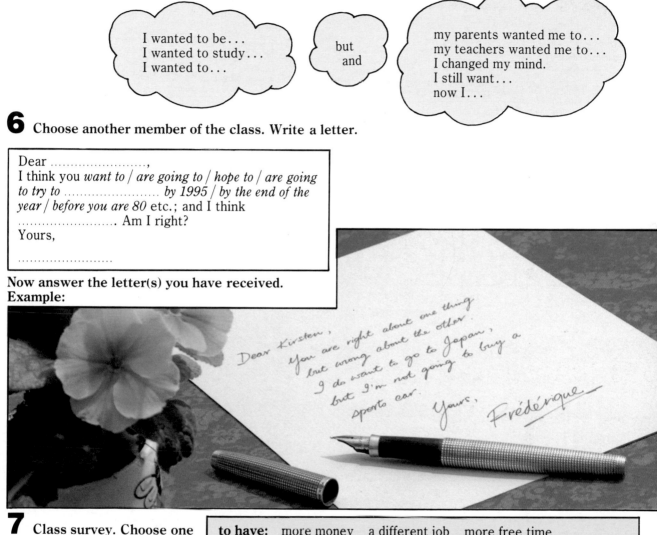

Dear Kirsten,
You are right about one thing but wrong about the other. I do want to go to Japan, but I'm not going to buy a sports car.
Yours, Frédérique

7 Class survey. Choose one of the things in the list and ask the other students if they would like it. Examples:

'Would you like to have a white Rolls Royce?'
'Yes, I would.'

'Would you like to be famous?'
'No, I certainly wouldn't.'

to have:	more money a different job more free time a better love-life (more) children more patience your picture in a magazine political power in your country a different house/flat more friends a private plane a white Rolls Royce a big motorbike two wives/husbands
to be:	famous an artist three years old
to:	sleep until midday every day live to be 100 speak a lot of languages travel a lot own a museum

8 Report the results of your survey. Examples:

'Three people out of twelve would like to travel a lot.'
'One person would like to be famous.'
'Everyone would like to speak a lot of languages.'

'Nobody would like to have a yacht.'
'Most people would like to have a private plane.'
'Not many people would like to live to be 100.'

B Could you do me a favour?

1 Complete the two conversations with the words and expressions in the boxes.

PAUL: Hey, John.
JOHN: Yeah?
PAUL: ....?
JOHN: Sure. What is it?
PAUL: Well, ..., I'm
.... until Friday.
........................, do you think?
JOHN: Yes, OK.
PAUL: ...., John. ....
JOHN: ....

the thing is   Thanks a lot
Could you do me a favour
That's all right   short of money
Could you lend me a fiver
That's very nice of you

ANNIE: ....
We've got a problem.
MR OLIVER: Oh yes? ....?
ANNIE: Well, ...,
.... We're cycling, and
we haven't got ....
tonight.
MR OLIVER: ....
the Crown Hotel?
ANNIE: Yes. It's .... too
expensive. So .... sleep
in your barn.
MR OLIVER: Yes, ...
.... You don't smoke,
do you?
ANNIE: Oh, no. Neither of us do. Well,
....
MR OLIVER: ....
come into the house for a wash?
ANNIE: ....
MR OLIVER: ....

Have you tried   much   all right   you see
Excuse me   Not at all   Would you like to
thank you very much   I don't mind
This way   I'm sorry to trouble you
What's the matter
I see   we wondered if we could
it's like this   anywhere to sleep
That's very kind of you

2 Can you find some examples of informal and formal language in the two conversations?

INFORMAL
Hey
Yeah?
. . .

FORMAL
Excuse me.
Oh, yes?
. . .

3 Practise the conversations with a partner.

4 Look at the pictures. In each picture, somebody wants somebody else to do something.
(i) Which pictures go with sentences 1–4? (ii) Listen to the four spoken sentences.
Which pictures go with them? (iii) Make sentences yourself for the last four pictures.

1. He wants them to sign a petition.
2. They want him to give them some water.
3. He wants her to take the dog for a walk.
4. He wants his father to lend him his car.

5 Pronunciation. Listen to the recording and write the words and expressions that you hear.

6 Work in pairs or groups of three. Make up a conversation for one of the pictures. Use some of the words and expressions from the conversations in Exercise 1.

Money

A Where does all the money go?

1 How much (approximately) is £1 in your currency? How much is £10? £50? $1? $20? $100? Make a note and try to remember. Then complete the table by guessing an amount for each blank. Listen to the recording and check your answers.

AVERAGE BRITISH HOUSEHOLD EXPENDITURE 1983	
(Pounds per week after taxes and insurance)	
Housing	£24.62
Fuel, electricity	7.24
Food	
Alcoholic drink	10.14
Tobacco	
Recreation, entertainment, education	13.03
Clothing, footwear	
Household goods and services	10.14
Other goods and services	17.38
Transport and communication	

2 Look at the table in Exercise 1 and answer the questions as quickly as you can.

1. What did the average family spend most on in 1983?
2. Which of the things in the table did they spend least on?
3. True or false? They spent more on alcohol than on heating and electricity.
4. Did they spend more on food than on housing?
5. Did they spend less on clothing than on transport and communication?
6. True or false? They spent nearly twice as much on alcohol as on tobacco.
7. True or false? Alcohol and tobacco together cost more than half as much as housing.

3 Say what you think about the figures in Exercise 1. Does the average British family spend too much on some things and not enough on others, in your opinion?

4 Make some sentences about your own expenditure this year, last year and next year. Examples:

'This year I've spent a lot of money on...'
I've spent too much on...'
I haven't spent much on...'

'Last year I spent a lot on...'
I spent too much on...'
I didn't spend much on...'

'This year I've spent less/more on...than last year.'
'Last year I spent less/more on...than this year.'

'I must spend less on...next year.'
'I can spend more on...next year.'

5 Budgets. Alice Calloway is a 25-year-old sales manager. She earns quite a good salary (you decide how much), and lives alone in a small flat. Work with another student and make a budget for Alice. You must decide how much she spends every week (in pounds or dollars) on the following items (you can add more if you want to).

rent	clothing and shoes
electricity and gas	alcohol
food and household	cigarettes
travel	entertainment
books	miscellaneous
telephone	savings

6 Cutting down expenditure. Alice has had to change her job for personal reasons. Her income is now 25% lower than it was. Exchange budgets with another pair of students. Your job now is to cut down Alice's expenditure by 25%. When you have done this, explain your changes to the two students who made the budget. Examples:

'We think Alice spends too much on...'
'She must spend less on...'
'She must travel less.'

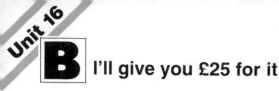

B I'll give you £25 for it

1 Listen to the conversation. Learn the new words and expressions. Then close your book, listen again, and try to write down the missing words.

A: How much do you want for it?
B: Forty.
A: Forty pounds?
B: Yes. It's worth fifty, but I'm in a hurry.
A: I don't know. It's not in very good condition. Look. This is broken. And look at this. I don't think it's worth forty. I'll give you twenty-five pounds.
B: Twenty-five? Come on. I'll tell you what – I'll take thirty-five. Since you're a friend of mine. You can have it for thirty-five.
A: No, that's still too much. To tell you the truth, I can't afford thirty-five.
B: I'm sorry. Thirty-five. That's my last word.
A: Come on, let's split the difference. Thirty pounds.
B: Thirty. Oh, very well. All right, thirty.
A: Can I give you a cheque?
B: Well, I'd prefer cash, if you don't mind.

2 Say these sentences from the dialogue. Remember to link the marked words.

How much do you want for it?
I'm in a hurry.
I don't know.
I don't think it's worth forty.
Since you're a friend of mine.
You can have it for thirty-five.
Come on, let's split the difference.
Can I give you a cheque?
Well, I'd prefer cash, if you don't mind.

3 Work with a partner. Each of you tries to sell something to the other, and you try to agree on a price. But you can't buy or sell until each of you has used at least two of the words or expressions you wrote down in Exercise 1.

4 Grammar revision. Put *too, too much* or *too many* in each blank.

1. 'How much are the carrots?' 'Forty pence a pound.' 'That's ....'
2. She doesn't go skiing any more. She's .... old.
3. You're driving .... fast. Please slow down.
4. If you eat .... chocolate, you'll get fat.
5. I've got .... books – I don't know where to put them all.
6. You've given me .... meat. I can't eat it all.

68

5 *Enough, not . . . enough or too?* Example:

1. too short OR not tall enough.

6 Copy the list of names; then listen to the recording of an auction. How much did each person pay?

Hunt Holtby Crowther Day Drew

Here is a list of some of the items sold at the auction. Listen again and match the items to the names of the people who bought them. There are some extra items.

a. Cigarette box, lighter and ashtray
b. Two boxes of miscellaneous
c. Espresso coffee maker
d. Blue and white bowl and cover
e. White chest of four drawers
f. Portable lights in excellent condition
g. Small bedroom chair

7 Ian and David have just rented a flat. They are going to an auction to buy some furniture. But they can't find anything they want. Match the sentences below with some of the lettered objects in the picture.

1. It's too heavy to carry.
2. It's too long to fit in the living room.
3. It's not big enough to hold all my books.
4. It's not strong enough to put anything on.
5. It's too difficult to clean.

Now imagine why Ian and David aren't buying some of the other things in the picture. Write two sentences with *too . . .* and two sentences with *not . . . enough*.

Before and after

A Do you get up as soon as you wake up?

1 Choose one of these questions (or make up a similar question) and ask as many people as possible. Make a note of the answers.

1. Do you get up as soon as you wake up?
2. Do you have breakfast before or after you get dressed?
3. Do you put your left shoe on before your right?
4. Do you make the bed before or after you have breakfast?
5. Do you undress before you brush your teeth at night?
6. Do you put the light out before or after you get into bed?
7. Do you go to bed at a fixed time, or do you wait until you're tired?
8. Before you go to sleep, do you usually read in bed?
9. Do you pay bills as soon as you get them?
10. Before you buy something, do you always ask the price?
11. Do you put salt on food before or after you taste it?
12. Do you read the newspaper before or after you arrive at work?
13. Do you address an envelope before or after you close it up?
14. Do you answer letters as soon as you get them?
15. Do you wait until your hair is too long before you go to the hairdresser?
16. Do you have to translate English sentences before you can understand them?
17. What are you going to do after the lesson has finished?
18. Are you going to study English before you go to bed tonight?
19. Will you study any more languages after you have learnt English?
20. Will you keep on working until you're 60?

2 Report the answers to the class.
Examples:

'Four students out of twelve have breakfast before they get dressed.'
'Sixty per cent of the students read the newspaper after they arrive at work.'
'Most people put their left shoe on before their right.'

3 How do you usually spend the evening? Write a paragraph using this skeleton.

When I ...., I .... Then
I .... and .... After that
I .... Then I .... until
.... Before I ...., I
....

4 Pronunciation. Say these words.

1. possible   on   long   not   stop   want
2. before   more   report   always   salt   saw   course   caught   bought
3. note   go   envelope   close   coat

Now put these words into groups 1, 2 or 3. (One word does not belong in any of the groups.)

no   off   short   got   home   other   fall   thought   draw   lost   horse   open   boat   gone   don't

Can you find any more words to put in the three groups?

5 Look at picture 1 and study the examples. Then put *still*, *yet* or *already* into the sentences.

1

John's still in bed.
He hasn't got up yet.
Susan is already dressed.

The postman has .... been.
Jane hasn't picked up her letters ....
They are .... on the mat.

Alice's taxi is .... waiting in front of her house.
Alice isn't ready ....
She is .... in the bath.

'Have you had lunch .... ?'
'No, I'm .... working. What about you?'
'I've .... eaten.'

Peter and Ann are both 19.
Ann is .... at school.
Peter is .... married.
He hasn't got any children ....

Jake is nearly 40, but he .... plays football every Saturday.
His son Andy is not 15 .... , but he is a good footballer, too.

6 Listen to the conversation between a commercial traveller and his boss. The traveller has to visit five places: Birmingham, Coventry, Dudley, Leamington and Wolverhampton (not in that order). Can you list the towns in the order in which he has visited them or will visit them?

7 Read the story.

ALISON BOGLE

Chapter 1
Alison Bogle lived in Exeter and worked in a bookshop. She was 23 – slim and pretty, rather shy and very quiet. She spent most of her spare time reading; at the weekend she went walking on the moors, or drove over to see her parents in Taunton.

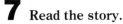

Alison was quite happy, but sometimes she wished she didn't have such a quiet life. Exeter was not really a very exciting place. At half past ten at night, all the lights went out. Nobody ever danced in the streets – at least, Alison had never seen it happen. And it rained all the time. *All* the time.

There were so many things Alison would like to do. So many things she hadn't done. For example, she had never been in an aeroplane.

Chapter 2
....
....
....

Chapter 3
Alison poured herself another glass of champagne and smiled at Carlos. What a man! He was so handsome. And such a good dancer. And so kind to her. Alison had never met anybody like him. She wondered what he was thinking.

The sun, shining down through the palm trees, made a moving pattern of light and shade on the sand. Carlos smiled back at her and stood up. He took her hand. 'Come on, let's have another swim,' he said.

8 Work with two or three other students. Make up Chapter 2 of the story. Then tell your Chapter 2 to another group.

B I hadn't seen her for a very long time

1 Choose the correct words and expressions to put in the gaps.

I .... down the street one day   *walked / was walking*
Looking at the shops
When someone asked me if I .... the way.   *know / knew*
I gave the girl directions
And then saw who it was.
I couldn't .... of anything to say.   *think / to think*

I hadn't seen her .... a very long time   *since / for*
Since the day we said goodbye.
She .... changed,   *hasn't / hadn't*
She .... looked young and shy.   *still / yet*
I thought perhaps .... changed so much   *I / I'd*
She didn't .... it was me,   *realise / realised*
Then I saw the recognition in her eye.

We stood in silence for a while,
Then I led her to a bar.
I felt as if I .... with a ghost.   *was walking / had walked*
We drank and began to talk
And then her eyes met mine.
Her eyes .... always shown her feelings most.   *have / had*

We .... about the good old days   *talked / have talked*
About family and friends
About the hopes we'd shared .... it all went   *before / after*
   wrong.
She seemed quite pleased to see me
So I .... two more drinks,   *ordered / had ordered*
But when I got back to the table she .... gone.   *has / had*

I hadn't seen her for a very long time *etc.*

2 Listen to the song and check your answers.

3 Past perfect tense. Look at the examples and then do the exercise.

PAST (THEN):	I **saw** who it was.
EARLIER PAST (BEFORE THEN):	I **hadn't seen** her for a very long time.
PAST·	We **talked** about...
EARLIER PAST:	...the hopes we'**d shared**.

Put in the correct tense (simple past or past perfect).

1. When we .... talking, I realised that we .... before. (*start; meet*)
2. When I .... at my suitcase, I could see that somebody .... to open it. (*look; try*)

3. When we got to the restaurant, we found that nobody .... to reserve a table. (*remember*)
4. The doctor ....him, and found that he .... his arm. (*examine; break*)
5. Before my 18th birthday I .... out of England. (*not be*)
6. We were a few minutes late, so the film .... when we .... to the cinema. (*already start; get*)
7. When she got to England, she found that the language was quite different from the English that she .... at school. (*learn*)
8. 'Good afternoon. Can I help you?' 'Yes. I .... my watch to you for repair three weeks ago. Is it ready yet?' (*bring*)

4 Pronunciation. Listen to the recording. How many words do you hear in each sentence? What are they? (Contractions like *I'd* count as two words.)

5 Listen to the story and then put the pictures in the right order.

6 Can you talk about one of these?

1. A day in your life when everything went wrong.
2. A meeting with somebody that you hadn't seen for a very long time.

Facts and opinions

A They thought the sun went round the earth

1 What did people believe hundreds of years ago?
Make sentences.

'They used to think that...'

the sun	was flat
the sky	could be made into gold
the earth	were born from mud
heavy things	was the centre of intelligence
lead	was made of crystal
the heart	went round the earth
insects	fell faster than light things

Do you know any other strange things that people used to believe?
Did you believe any strange things when you were a child?

2 Who found out what?

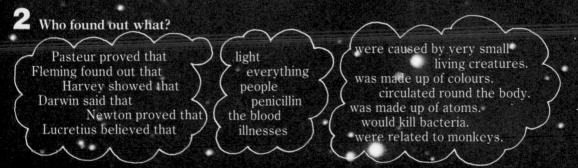

Pasteur proved that	light	were caused by very small living creatures.
Fleming found out that	everything	was made up of colours.
Harvey showed that	people	circulated round the body.
Darwin said that	penicillin	was made up of atoms.
Newton proved that	the blood	would kill bacteria.
Lucretius believed that	illnesses	were related to monkeys.

Can you think of other things that famous scientists have found out?

3 Pronunciation. Say these sentences with the correct stress.

1. People **thought** that the **earth** was **flat**.
2. They be**lieved** that the **sky** was **solid**.
3. They **thought** that the **sun went round** the **earth**.

Where are the stresses in these sentences? Can you say them?

4. They thought that the stars were holes in the sky.
5. They didn't know that the sun was a star.
6. They believed that mountains were the homes of gods.

4 Change the quotations from direct speech to reported speech. Examples:

Marx: 'Religion is the opium of the people'.
'Marx said that religion was the opium of the people.'
The young George Washington: 'I cannot tell a lie'.
'Washington said that he could not tell a lie.'

1. Stevenson: 'To travel hopefully is better than to arrive'.
2. Dorothy Parker (of another woman): 'She speaks 18 languages, and she can't say "no" in any of them'.
3. Somebody (of President Gerald Ford): 'He can't walk and chew gum at the same time'.
4. Anita Loos: 'Gentlemen prefer blondes'.
5. Oscar Wilde: 'It is better to be beautiful than to be good'.
6. The British Prime Minister Harold Wilson: 'A week is a long time in politics'.
7. Calderon: 'Life is a dream'.
8. *The Daily Express* in 1938: 'There will be no war in Europe'.
9. Dr Dionysus Lardner (1793–1859): 'Rail travel at high speed is impossible because people will not be able to breathe'.
10. Professor J.H. Pepper: 'The electric light has no future'.
11. Simon Newcomb, American astronomer: 'Artificial flight is impossible'.
12. Professor Tait: 'The telephone is physically impossible'.
13. Admiral Leahy, US Navy, June 1945: 'The atom bomb will never go off, and I speak as an expert in explosives'.

5 Listen to the recording and try to complete the sentences. The words in the box will help you.

> light   right   ring   satellite   speed
> telescope   true   wrong

1. The ancient Greek philosopher Aristotle said that heavy things fell...
2. For 2,000 years everybody believed that Aristotle...
3. In the 16th century, scientists started to wonder if Aristotle's beliefs...
4. The Italian scientist Galileo did some experiments which proved that Aristotle...
5. He showed that heavy things...
6. Galileo was the first person to...
7. He found out that Jupiter...
8. and that Saturn...
9. and that there were mountains...
10. and spots...

6 Work in groups of about four. Prepare some 'general knowledge' questions to ask other students. Begin *Do you know...?* or *Can you tell me...?* Examples:

'Do you know if gold is heavier than lead?'
'Can you tell me whether Britain has a king or a queen?'
'Do you know what his or her name is?'
'Do you know who Marco Polo was?'
'Can you tell me who Robert Redford is?'
'Do you know where the President was born?'
'Can you tell me who discovered radium?'
'Do you know who invented the telephone?'
'Do you know where Toronto is?'

B Probability

1 Look at the information about Fred Smith. Then listen to the recording of a conversation between Fred and a girl at a party. What did he say that was not true? Example:

'Fred said that he lived in Paris and California.'
'He told the girl that he had been to Venice.'

FRED SMITH
Full name: Frederick George Smith.
Age: 25
Address: 17 Victoria Terrace, Highbury, London N5.
Profession: van driver.
Interests: photography, model aeroplanes.
Education: Finsbury Park Comprehensive School.
Qualifications: none
Father: Albert Eric Smith, 52, shop assistant.
Mother: Florence Anne Smith, née Henderson, 48, housewife.

2 Here are some of the things that Fred said in the conversation. Do you think they are true? Use one of the expressions in the box.

It must be true.	It's probably true.
It could be true.	It might be true.
It's probably not true.	It can't be true.

1. My friends call me Fred.
2. I photograph famous people.
3. I travel all over the world.
4. I've been photographing the President for *Time* magazine.
5. Famous people are all the same.
6. I find you interesting.
7. I want to photograph you.
8. I love poetry.

LLANDYFRDWY

3 Look at the picture. What can you say about the time and place? Examples:

'It might be morning, because . . .'
'It can't be in Germany, because . . .'
'It must be during the day, because . . .'

76

4 Pronunciation. Say these words.

1. star   stop   stand   studio   start   student
2. speak   spoke   Spain   spend
3. score   Scotland   Scottish
4. spring   spread   strange   street   straight
   screw   scratch   scream

5 Look at the examples to see how *likely* is used.

She **is likely to** come soon. = She **will probably** come soon.
I **am likely to** need help. = I **will probably** need help.

Now express these ideas using *likely*.

1. I will probably go to Spain soon.
2. She will probably spend next week in London.
3. It will probably stop raining soon.
4. You will probably meet some strange people at John's house.
5. If you start learning English now, you will probably speak it quite well by next summer.
6. They say the spring will probably be wet this year.

Now look at these examples.

There is likely to be a phone call for me.
   = **There will probably be** a phone call for me.
There are likely to be about 20 people at the party. = **There will probably be** about 20 people at the party.

Now express these ideas using *there is/are likely to be...*

1. There will probably be an election in June.
2. There will probably be some problems.
3. There will probably be snow in Scotland.
4. There will probably be a parking place in this street.

6 What is likely to happen in your life? In your country? In the world? Make sentences with *likely*.

7 Reading and dictionary use.

1. **Read the text and write down the words you don't know. Do *not* use a dictionary.**
2. **Read the text again. How well can you understand it? (*Very well/quite well/not very well/not at all*.)**
3. **Look at the words you wrote down. Have you got any idea what some of them mean? Look at the text and see if you can guess.**
4. **Which of the words do you really need to look up in a dictionary, to understand the text well? Look them up and read the text once more.**
5. **Choose some of the new words to learn.**

THE AMAZON FOREST AND THE FUTURE OF THE WORLD

The Amazon forest, in Brazil, covers five million square kilometres – an area as big as the whole of Europe excluding Russia. It contains one third of the world's trees.

However, the trees are disappearing. By 1974, a quarter of the forest had already been cut down. In the following year, 1975, 4% of the remaining trees went. If the destruction of the forest continues at the same rate, there will be nothing left by the year 2005.

Scientists say that the disappearance of the trees is already causing changes in the climate. In Peru, there is less snow than before on the high peaks of the Andes mountains. In Bolivia, there is less rain than before and more wind. In some parts of north-east Brazil there is now very little rain.

What will happen if more of the Amazon forest is cut down? According to climatologists, two things are likely to happen: there will be serious effects on the world's climate, and the air that we breathe will lose some of its oxygen. Why is this?

Trees absorb the gas carbon dioxide from the air, and give out oxygen into the air. The trees of the Amazon rain forest are chemically very active, and some scientists believe that they provide 50% of the world's annual production of oxygen. If we lose the tropical forests, the air will contain much less oxygen and much more carbon dioxide. It will become difficult – perhaps even impossible – to breathe.

With more carbon dioxide in the air, the temperature will rise; the ice-caps at the North and South Poles will melt; the sea level will rise, and hundreds of coastal cities will be flooded.

Scientists do not all agree about the exact figures – the calculations can be done in different ways with different results. But all scientists agree that if we destroy the Amazon forest it will be environmental suicide – like losing an ocean. Life on earth will become difficult, and it may become impossible.

Small talk

A Hello, nice to see you

1 Listen to Dialogue 1, and write the numbers and letters of the expressions you hear.

1. A I go.
   B I'm going.
   C I'll go.

2. A Nice to see you.
   B It's nice to see you.
   C Nice seeing you.

3. A Are we late?
   B We're late.
   C Aren't we late?

4. A You're first
   B You're the first
   C You're not first

5. A Who is coming?
   B Who ever's coming?
   C Who else is coming?

6. A Can I take your coat?
   B Let me take your coat.
   C Shall I take your coat?

7. A You know Lucy, do you?
   B You know Lucy, don't you?
   C You don't know Lucy, do you?

8. A I think we've met her once.
   B I think we met her once.
   C I think we'll meet her one day.

9. A What can I get you to drink?
   B What can I give you to drink?
   C What would you like to drink?

10. A The room doesn't look nice, John.
    B The room does look nice, John.
    C Doesn't the room look nice, John?

11. A You've changed it about
    B You've changed it round
    C You've changed it over

2 Listen again. Which of these do you hear?

A don't you? D wasn't it?
B do you? E aren't we?
C isn't it? F haven't you?

3 Real questions or not? Listen to the sentences. Does the voice go up or down at the end? Examples:

The piano was over by the window, wasn't it?
You know Lucy, don't you?

1. It's a lovely day, isn't it?
2. You're French, aren't you?
3. She's got fatter, hasn't she?
4. The train leaves at 4.13, doesn't it?
5. Children always like cartoon films, don't they?
6. It's your birthday next week, isn't it?
7. Hotels are expensive here, aren't they?
8. Ann said she'd phone, didn't she?

4 Work with two or three other students. Act out a 'greeting' scene like the one in Dialogue 1.

5 Listen to Dialogue 2. Then look at the following sentences. Are they true or false? Write 'T' (true), 'F' (false), or 'DK' (don't know).

1. Lucy works in a pub.
2. She likes her work.
3. She doesn't meet many interesting people.
4. Lucy's job is always hard work.
5. There is only one barman in her pub.
6. John works in a bank.
7. He likes his job very much.
8. He has just been made manager.
9. He's going to move to another town soon.
10. Lucy wouldn't like to move to another town.
11. John has lived in the same place for six years.

6 Listen again. Can you remember some sentences from the dialogue?

7 Real questions. Listen and repeat.

1. That's hard work, isn't it?
2. You're an accountant, aren't you?
3. You have to move round, don't you?
4. It'll be in another town, won't it?

8 Asking for agreement. Listen and repeat.

1. It's a nice day, isn't it?
2. She's very pretty, isn't she?
3. Good clothes are expensive, aren't they?
4. You're tired, aren't you?

9 Work with four or five other students. You are all in the same compartment on a long train journey. Act out a conversation in which you get to know one another.

10 Listen to Dialogue 3. Write down all the words you hear for things that you can eat or drink.

11 Can you complete these questions from the dialogue?

What are you looking ....?
What are John and Lucy talking ....?

Now read the following answers and write the questions.

1. They're talking about politics.
   What are they talking about?
2. I went with Henry.
3. I'm looking for Alice.
4. I bought it for you.
5. I'm thinking about holidays.
6. I'm listening to some piano music.
7. I'm looking at your ear-rings.
8. The letter was from Andy.

12 Asking for agreement. Listen, and say the 'question-tags'. Example:

It's a nice day, ...

... isn't it?

B I didn't think much of it

1 Listen to Dialogue 4.
What do you think they were
talking about?
Can you remember any of the
things they said?

2 Which of these words and expressions come in the dialogue?
Write down your answers; then listen again and see if you were
right.

I liked it all   lovely   nonsense   I didn't think much of it
I cried   I couldn't help it   It made him laugh
It didn't say anything to me   I may be very old-fashioned
So am I   I like violence   Why did you like it?
It was really really boring   three old men   Who wrote it?
I've never heard of him

3 Write down the names of a food, a sport,
an animal and a person (singer, actor,
writer, ...) that you like. Tell another student,
and listen to his or her answers.

I like ...
I quite like ...
  I really like ...
I like ... very much.
  I love ...

So do I.
I don't.
  I quite like him/her/
  it/them.
I've never heard of
him/her/it/them.

Write down the names of a food, a sport, an
animal and a person (singer, actor, writer, ...)
that you don't like.
Tell another student and listen to his or her
answers.

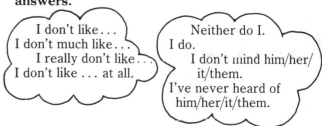

I don't like ...
I don't much like ...
  I really don't like ...
I don't like ... at all.

Neither do I.
I do.
  I don't mind him/her/
  it/them.
I've never heard of
him/her/it/them.

4 Write down the names of three books/films/plays etc. that you liked and three that you didn't.
Tell other students and listen to their answers.

> I liked...
> I really liked...
> etc.

> So did I.
> I didn't.
> I didn't think much
> of it.
> I haven't seen it.
> I've never heard of it.
> etc.

> I didn't like...
> I didn't much like...
> etc.

> Neither did I.
> I did.
> I quite liked it.
> I haven't read it.
> etc.

5 Talk some more about books/plays/films etc. that you have read or seen.

6 Listen to Dialogue 5. The following sentences are like sentences in the dialogue, but they are not exactly the same.
What are the exact sentences in the dialogue?

It's late.
We've got to go a long way.
We'd better go, too.
Thank you very much, Ann.
I really enjoyed myself.
Thanks for coming.
You must come and see us soon.
I'll phone you.
This isn't mine.
Well, who is this, then?
It's old and dirty.

7 Look at the dialogue texts on pages 156–158.
Choose a sentence and try to say it with a good pronunciation.
The teacher will say it for you correctly.

8 Listen to Dialogues 1–5 again.
Read the texts, and write down some useful expressions to learn.

9 Improvisation. Work in groups of six to eight. Act out a dinner party. How long can you go on for?

Do it

A How to do it

1 Match the words and the pictures.

| cover | peel | rub |
| scratch | shake | stick |

2 Here are some useful practical tips for everyday life. Unfortunately, the beginnings and ends have got mixed up. Can you sort them out?

To make tomatoes easier to peel,
If you want to pick up a rabbit,
To get cigarette stains off your fingers,

If you catch German measles,

You can clean dirty saucepans

To get dust out of a guitar,
If two glasses are stuck together,

To get small scratches off your watch glass,
You can make tight shoes more comfortable

rub them with lemon first and then wash them.
rub it with liquid brass cleaner.
cover them with very hot water for a minute or two.
put cold water in one and stand the other in hot water.
by packing them with wet newspaper and leaving them overnight.
don't hold its ears.
don't visit anyone who is pregnant unless you're sure she's already had them.
put rice inside it, shake it and empty it.
by filling them with cold water and vinegar and letting them boil for five minutes.

3 How do you think these tips begin?

... don't put your address on the outside of your
luggage.
... by rubbing it with a cut potato or apple.
... put a glass of beer a few yards away.
... hold the back over the steam from a kettle.

4 Can you complete these tips?

The night before an examination, ...
To find out how far away a thunderstorm is, ...
You can get a tight ring off by ...

5 Work in groups. Each group writes four
tips (serious or funny ones). Then copy the tips,
with the beginnings and ends out of order, and
give them to another group to put in order.

6 Say these words. Notice the stress.

1. side   ex**ci**ting   said   ex**cept**
2. pen   spend   ex**pen**sive   speak
   ex**pe**rience   sport   **ex**port
3. rest   press   ex**pre**ssion
4. late   play   ex**plain**
5. shave   change   ex**change**

7 Imagine your plane has just crashed on an
island where no one lives. You may not be
rescued for months. Talk about what there is to
do. Examples:

'We'd better build a place to sleep in.'
'We should make a fire that planes can see.'

8 Work with six or seven other students.
Make a plan for the class's life on the island.
Decide who should do what part of the work
and why, and report to the class. Examples:

*'We think Giovanna should plan the houses, because
she's an architect.'*
*'Ahmed had better not do any hard work, because
he's been ill.'*

B If I were you,...

1 Match the expressions and the pictures.

> back to front   face downwards   inside out
> sideways   underneath   upside down

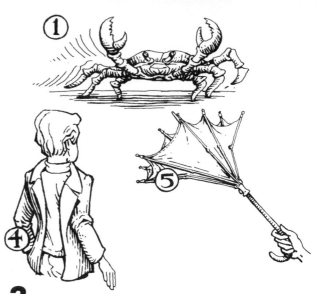

2 Listen to the dialogue. Are there any differences between the version on the recording and the version in the book?

A: If I were you, I'd turn it the other way round.
B: Well, I think I'll try it this way first.
A: I mean, –
C: Hello. I wouldn't do it like that if I were you.
B: Wouldn't you?
C: No, I think you ought to turn it upside down.
B: Oh, really? I'll think about it.
C: Yes, and put a blanket underneath first, or it'll get dirty.
D: Hi. Why don't you turn it sideways?
B: You think so?
D: Oh, yes, and remember to cover it, or it'll get wet.
B: Get wet?
A: You really ought to take the wheels off first, you know.
B: Well, I –
E: I think it would be much better if he turned it back to front, don't you?
A: That's just what I said.
D: Don't forget to tighten all the screws up.
C: You're not getting anywhere like that.
D: If I were you, I'd go back to the beginning and start again.
C: And I still think you should turn it upside down.
E: Let's help him.
B: It's quite all right. I can do it by myself, thank you very much.
E: No, it's no trouble.
A: Come on, everybody.

3 Look through the dialogue and write down some useful expressions and structures to learn.
Exchange lists with one or more other students and see if you have thought of the same expressions.

4 Fluency practice. Choose a sentence from the dialogue and practise saying it. Try for accurate intonation and rhythm.

5 Put a verb from the box into each blank (or set of blanks). Use some verbs more than once; use the correct tenses.

> be   change   do   explain   have   know
> look   make   read   ring   stop   take

A: I don't know what to do. If John _were_ here, he ....
B: Yeah, if John .... here, he .... what to do, but .... he .... how to do it? If I .... you, I' .... the instructions again.
A: I've read them twice already. Do you think it .... a good idea if I .... the top off and .... inside?
B: I don't know. I don't think I' .... that if it .... mine.
A: Wouldn't you? What .... you .... if you .... this mess in your kitchen?
B: I' .... worrying about it for the moment; I' .... Pat and .... the problem; I' .... my plans for this evening.
A: Yeah, I suppose you're right. If I .... the top off, I' .... probably just .... it worse. Pour me a drink while I ring Pat, will you?

6 Four friends wrote to Christine asking for advice. Here are bits of their letters and bits of her answers. Match the problem to the answer.
Then work in groups: imagine one of the situations and invent the rest of Christine's letter. Try to use some of the expressions you have learnt in this lesson.

has ever been in trouble with the law befor

the only time I've been interested in another man, and it's finished now. Should I tell Steve or

parents just don't understand. Just because he's younger than me, they think

must be drugs. She won't talk to us about it, and we don't know who to

you, I would go to the family doctor immediately

were you, I wouldn't say anything to him. I've known him since long before you were married,

as bad as it seems. If you can't afford a good lawyer, she ought to be able to get one free by

Why don't I talk to your mother? Perhaps her feelings wouldn't get in the way so much if I spoke to her

7 Pronunciation. Say these words.

1. ask   asks
2. ghost   ghosts   post   posts
3. find   finds   mend   mends   sound   sounds
4. tap   taps   envelope   envelopes
5. bank   banks   drink   drinks
6. aunt   aunts   invent   invents
7. tap   tapped   hope   hoped   help   helped
8. like   liked   work   worked   sack   sacked
9. isn't   doesn't   wasn't   hasn't
10. hadn't   wouldn't   couldn't   shouldn't

8 Prepare a short speech (maximum two minutes). In your speech, you must try to make other students do something. For example: stop studying English; leave the room; give up smoking; become vegetarians; change their religion; give you a lot of money; buy you a car; change their jobs.

Technology

A Electricity

1 Look at the pictures. Do you know the names of some of these things? Work in groups of three or four and try to list as many as possible.

2 In all of these words, the last syllable is pronounced /ə/. Look at the spellings. Then say the words after the recording or your teacher.

heater cooker computer calculator
transistor mirror similar sugar
centre theatre departure figure
there here where hear wear hair
their Africa cinema idea visa

3 If you could have just five of the things in the picture (plus leads, plugs and sockets), which would you choose? Which five are the least important?

4 Which of the things in the picture can you see now? Which of them are somewhere else in the building?

5 Look at the pictures below and listen to the recording. Which thing is described in each sentence? Example:

It's plugged in and switched on. It's black and white.   *The radio.*

6 Look at the sentences and say what you should do. Use these verbs.

| switch on | switch off | turn up |
| turn down | plug in | unplug |

Example:

What should you do if you've finished using your calculator? *'Switch it off.'*

What should you do if:
1. the radio isn't loud enough?
2. the record player's too loud?
3. you see in the newspaper that there's an interesting TV programme just starting?
4. you don't want to watch TV any more?
5. the TV's on fire?
6. the cooker's too hot?
7. you want to use your calculator?
8. the iron isn't getting the creases out of your clothes?
9. the iron's burning your clothes?
10. you've finished with the iron?

7 Put in *should, shouldn't, must* or *mustn't.*

1. You .... always switch electrical appliances off when you are not using them.
2. Small children .... watch violent programmes on TV.
3. In Britain, before you start using a new electrical appliance, you .... put the right kind of plug on.
4. When you put a plug on, you .... be careful to put the wires in the right places.
5. You .... touch electrical appliances when you are in the bath.
6. When you move into a new house or flat, you .... check the electrical wiring.
7. You .... plug too many things into the same socket.
8. You .... wash white and coloured clothes separately.
9. You .... clean out the fridge from time to time.
10. You .... let the iron get too hot if you are ironing silk.
11. You .... turn your radio up loud at night.
12. In Britain, you .... buy a licence every year if you have a TV.

8 Look at the information and then answer these questions.
1. **How much would your use of electricity cost you every week if you paid British prices?**
2. **Which electrical appliance do people in the class spend the most money on?**
3. **Who spends the most on electricity?**

THE COST OF ELECTRICITY
1. Electricity is sold by the 'unit'. (You use one unit if you use 1 kilowatt [1,000 watts] of electricity for one hour, or 500 watts for 2 hours, or 100 watts for 10 hours.)
2. In Britain in 1984, one unit cost about 5p.
3. To see what you get for one unit, look at the information below.

WHAT YOU GET FOR ONE UNIT
electric blanket: 2 nights
convector heater: ½ hour
food mixer: over 60 cakes
hair dryer: 3 hours
iron: over 2 hours
kettle: 12 pints of water (7 litres)
light (100w bulb or 1,500mm tube): 10 hours
radio: 30 hours
record player: over 24 hours
fridge: 1 day

clothes dryer (tumble dryer): ½ hour
stereo: 8–10 hours
tape recorder: over 24 hours
black and white TV: 9 hours
colour TV: 6 hours
toaster: 70 slices of toast
vacuum cleaner: 2–4 hours cleaning
electric razor: 3,000 shaves
hot water: 1 bath, 4 showers or 10 bowls of washing-up water

LARGER APPLIANCES
cooker: it takes 20–25 units to cook one week's meals for a family of four.
dishwasher: one full load uses 2½ units.
freezer: ½ unit per 10 litres per week.
washing machine: it takes 9 units to do the weekly wash for a family of four.

B It doesn't work

1 Match the objects with the problems. You can use a dictionary. The first two answers are done for you.

a. It makes a funny noise. *2,4,7,9*

b. It won't start. *4,7*

c. It won't wind on.

d. It doesn't work.

e. The dial's broken.

f. It won't record.

g. It's started going very fast.

h. It won't stop dripping.

i. One of the buttons is stuck.

j. It won't turn off.

k. I can't hear anything.

l. It smells funny.

m. There's no colour.

n. It keeps flooding.

o. There's something wrong with the engine.

p. It won't ring.

q. It's stopped.

r. It's leaking.

s. The rewind's stuck.

t. It's slow.

u. The flash won't work properly.

v. It keeps sticking.

2 Put in an infinitive or an *-ing* form.

1. My watch has stopped .... (*work*)
2. I would like .... a better stereo. (*buy*)
3. I very much enjoy .... photos of animals. (*take*)
4. Do you like .... sport on TV? (*watch*)
5. I must ask Harry .... my cassette player. (*mend*)
6. We hope .... a new car soon. (*get*)
7. I don't want .... Judy – will you do it? (*telephone*)
8. Our dishwasher keeps .... (*flood*)
9. Thanks very much for .... my bicycle. (*mend*)
10. Don't forget .... some oil in the car. (*put*)
11. I can't stand .... advertisements on TV. (*watch*)
12. We must .... the mixer back to the shop – it doesn't work. (*take*)

3 Listen to the recording. How many words do you hear in each sentence? What are they? (Contractions like *What's* count as two words.)

88

4 Look these words up in a dictionary or ask your teacher what they mean.

guarantee   pressure   pressure cooker receipt   release   stainless steel

Now listen to the telephone conversation and answer these questions.

1. Is the pressure cooker stainless steel?
2. Is it automatic?
3. What's the problem?
4. Is it under guarantee?
5. Can the man find the guarantee papers?
6. Does the man have the receipt?
7. What is the man's name?
8. Where does the man live: East Hagby, East Hadley or East Hagbourne?
9. Does the woman think she can help him?
10. How long has he had the pressure cooker?
11. What make is it?
12. About how much did the pressure cooker cost?

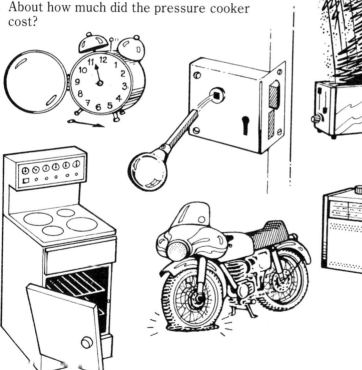

5 Work with a partner, and make up a conversation about something that has gone wrong. You can talk about one of the things in Exercise 1, about one of the things in the pictures on this page, or about something else if you prefer.
Use some of the expressions from Exercise 1, and some of these expressions from the telephone conversation.

Can I help you?	What make is it?
I hope so.	Is it under guarantee?
I've got a problem with…	I'll take your name.
How long have you had it?	Thank you very much for your help.

89

Revision and fluency practice

A A choice of activities

> Look at the exercises in this lesson. Try to decide which of them are most useful for you, and do one or more.

LISTENING

1 Listen to the recording. You will hear some sentences with mistakes in. Answer by saying the correct sentences (below) with the right stress. Examples:

'You lost a briefcase, didn't you?'
*'No, I **found** a briefcase.'*

'Sally found a briefcase, didn't she?'
*'No, **I** found a briefcase.'*

'You found a handbag, didn't you?'
*'No, I found a **briefcase**.'*

1. No, I found a briefcase.
2. No, my mother lives in London.
3. No, it's John's birthday on Tuesday.
4. No, I'm a teacher of German and Arabic.
5. No, I live at 37 Edinburgh Road.

2 Listen to the football results and answer the questions.

1. Did Manchester City win?
2. Who lost against Swansea?
3. How many goals did Manchester United score?
4. What was the score between Liverpool and Arsenal?
5. Did Nottingham Forest play at home or away?
6. How many draws were there?

3 Try to fill in the missing words. Then listen to the song and see if you were right.

A BIGGER HEART

His arms are stronger than mine
His legs are ..:......... than mine
His car's always cleaner
And his grass is always ....

But my heart is .... than his
And my love for you is stronger than his.

His shirts are .... than mine
His soufflés are lighter than mine
His video is ....
And his faults are fewer

But my heart is .... than his
And my love for you is stronger than his.

He's more ...., much more elegant
More charming and polite than me
He's more responsible, much more dependable
He's everything I long to be.

His office is .... than mine
His martinis are drier than mine
His roses are ....
And his overdraft is smaller

But my heart is .... than his
And my love for you is stronger than his.

SPELLING AND PRONUNCIATION

4 Do you know how to pronounce these words?

Two syllables, not three: asp(i)rin, bus(i)ness, cam(e)ra, diff(e)rent, ev(e)ning, ev(e)ry, marri(a)ge, med(i)cine.

Three syllables, not four: comf(or)table, secret(a)ry, temp(e)rature, veg(e)table, usu(a)lly.

Silent letters: shou(l)d, cou(l)d, wou(l)d, ca(l)m, wa(l)k, ta(l)k, ha(l)f, i(r)on, i(s)land, lis(t)en, (w)rite, (w)rong, (k)now, (k)nife, (k)nee, (k)nock, (k)nob, dau(gh)ter, hei(gh)t, li(gh)t, mi(gh)t, ri(gh)t, ti(gh)t, strai(gh)t, throu(gh), wei(gh), nei(gh)bour, ou(gh)t, thou(gh)t, g(u)ess, g(u)ide, g(u)itar, (h)our, (h)onest, We(d)n(e)sday, san(d)wich, si(g)n.

(For a more complete list of spelling and pronunciation problems, see the Summary.)

90

SPEAKING

5 Question-box. Take a question out of the box, read it aloud and answer it. Say at least one sentence; if you like, you can say more. If you don't like a question, you can say *I'd rather not answer*, but you must take another question and answer it.

6 The *yes/no* game. Work in groups. One person has to answer questions for one minute; the others ask him or her as many questions as possible. The person who answers must not say *yes* or *no*.

READING

7 Use your dictionary and get rich. Look at the paper and the map, and try to decide where the money is buried. You can look up *four* words (maximum) in your dictionary. Which four words will you look up?

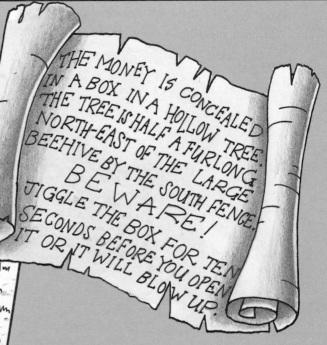

THE MONEY IS CONCEALED IN A BOX IN A HOLLOW TREE. THE TREE IS HALF A FURLONG NORTH-EAST OF THE LARGE BEEHIVE BY THE SOUTH FENCE. B E W A R E ! JIGGLE THE BOX FOR TEN SECONDS BEFORE YOU OPEN IT OR IT WILL BLOW UP.

8 Read this text and write down the words you don't know.
How well can you understand the text without looking up the words?
Can you guess what any of the words mean?
How many of the words do you *have* to look up?
Look them up and read the text again.

BLACKBEARD'S TREASURE

In the 17th century Spanish ships sailed regularly to Central and South America to fetch gold for the Spanish government. The ships were often attacked by pirates, who infested the 'Spanish Main' (the sea area north-east of Central and South America).

As the pirates could obviously not bank their stolen gold, they buried it. A famous pirate called Blackbeard, who operated on the Spanish Main from 1690 to 1710, hid his treasure somewhere on the coast of North Carolina. He then killed everyone who knew where the treasure was, and boasted 'Only the Devil and myself know the hiding place'.

Perhaps the Devil told somebody, because it seems likely that Blackbeard's treasure was dug up on Christmas Day 1928, at a place called Plum Point in North Carolina. But the gold disappeared again at once: nobody knows who found it, or where it has gone.

B What do you say when you...?

1 Here are some pairs of sentences. In each pair, the two sentences mean the same, but one is more formal than the other. Can you divide them into formal and informal?

Hello. ......*F*.......

Hi. ....*I*.......

How's it going?
How are you?

Can't complain.
Very well, thank you.

Goodbye.
See you.

Hey!
Excuse me.

Have you got a fiver?
Could you lend me five pounds?

Thank you very much.
Thanks a lot.

Do you mind if I smoke?
Is it OK if I smoke?

How much is that?
What do you want for that?

2 Can you match the expressions and the situations?
Example:

'Can I look round?' Shop

EXPRESSIONS	SITUATIONS
Can I look round?	Shop
I'll put you through.	Doctor's surgery
Fill up with four-star, please.	Lost property office
A single for two nights.	Thanking somebody
Single to Manchester.	Making an appointment
Check in at 9.30.	On the telephone
Second on the left.	Pub
It was green, with a red handle.	Hotel reception
That's very kind of you.	Complaining about faulty goods
I'll give you twenty-five for it.	Garage / petrol station
Pint of bitter, please.	Bank
It won't switch off.	Replying to thanks
Could we make it a bit later?	Hairdresser
How would you like it?	Airport
It hurts when I bend down.	Giving directions
Not at all.	Bargaining
Not too short, please.	Station

3 Choose five of the situations and see if you can think of another typical expression for each one.

4 Work with two or three other students. Make a list of typical expressions for one of the situations. Your teacher will help you.
Useful questions:

How do you say...?
What do you say when...?
What's the English for...?
How do you pronounce...?
How do you spell...?
What does...mean?

5 Prepare and practise a conversation for the situation which you studied in Exercise 4.

93

Feelings

A Not exactly calm

1 Match the words with the faces. You can use your dictionary.

| afraid amused angry cross |
| pleased relaxed sad |
| surprised upset worried |

2 How many different words from Exercise 1 can you use to complete these sentences?

People frown when they're...

People smile when they're...

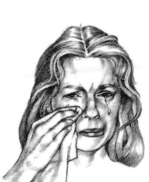

People cry when they're...

People laugh when they're...

3 Underline the stressed syllables, and then circle the vowels that are pronounced /ə/. Say the words after the recording or your teacher. Example:

(a)fraid

1. amused   surprised   correct   about
2. never   ever   problem   children

4 How might you feel if you said these things? Example:

What was that noise?   *surprised or afraid* ....

1. Where have you been?
2. Isn't this nice!
3. Damn you!
4. He should be more careful.
5. Oh dear!
6. What a lovely idea!
7. You're kidding!
8. You'd better not do that again.
9. I can't see a thing.

Now invent a short conversation using at least two of the sentences above.

5 Fill the blanks with the words from the box; you can use your dictionary. Then listen and see if you were right.

| anything   around   bad times   calm |
| cry   emotions   helped   imagined |
| inside   problem   quickly   upset |

I'm not exactly .... In fact, I'm a fairly emotional person. I express my .... easily, and never let them build up .... me. I enjoy the good times more, and get over the .... more ...., when I can talk or shout or .... about them. So the people .... me usually know what kind of mood I'm in. Strangely enough, this .... me keep a secret once. I had a .... that .... me terribly, and for once I didn't want to share it with anyone. No one ever .... that I was hiding ....!

6 Choose one of these questions to ask other students. Note the answers and report to the class.

Do you sometimes let small things upset you very much, or are you usually easy-going?
Do you ever let emotions build up inside you and then express them too strongly?
Do you usually let the people around you know how you feel about things?
Can you think of a time when you were very upset but didn't let anyone know?
Would you let your children know if you were very worried about something?
OR: Would you let your parents know if you were very worried about something?

B In love

1 Who loves who? Look at the picture and answer the questions as fast as you can.

1. Who does Janet love?
2. Who loves Janet?
3. Who does Eric love?
4. Who likes Eric?
5. Who dislikes Eric?
6. Who does Eric dislike?
7. Who loves Alice?
8. Who does Alice love?
9. Who does Janet hate?
10. Who hates Janet?
11. How does Eric feel about Philip?
12. Does Philip feel the same about him?
13. Do Philip and Janet love each other?

2 Listen to the recording. You will hear Philip, Eric, Alice and Janet (not in that order). Can you decide who you are listening to each time?

3 Pronounce these words and phrases after your teacher or the recording.

1. slowly   strongly   special   stand   smell
2. slowly   as slowly   not slowly
3. special   as special   had special
4. strongly   as strongly   not strongly
5. stand   she's standing   don't stand
6. smile   this smile   that smile

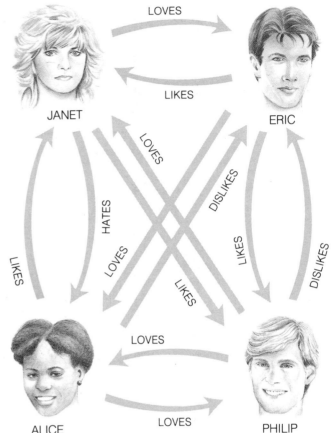

"This could be difficult. They say they're all together."

4 Here is a letter that Philip wrote to an advice programme on the radio. Read it without worrying about the blanks. How much can you understand – most, more than half, half, not much?

Dear Radio Helpline,

Please help me.   I have got a ...1... problem.   I am in love with two women at the same time!

I met Janet through my work about a year ago, and we began going out together.   I love and ...2... her a lot, and would like to think we might decide to spend our lives together.   We share so many things; it is a very special ...3...   She does not feel as strongly about me as I do about her, but she is certainly very ...4... of me.   We have been growing ...5... over the year, and I have been hoping that she will slowly realise how ...6... we are to be together.

Then, three weeks ago, at a party, I met Alice.   It was love at first sight – I feel as if I have known her all my life.   She is very much ...7... with me, too.   I have told her about Janet.

What should I do?   My problem must sound ...8... to some people, but it is not ...9... for me.   I think of both of them all the time.   The feeling I have for Alice is more exciting, but will it ...10...?   I haven't had the time to ...11... her very well yet.   Should I just wait and see what happens?   I feel a bit ...12... about the whole thing.   Please help.

Yours,

Philip

5 Here are the words that go in the blanks in Exercise 4. Try to put each word in the right place. One word is used twice.

admire	You *admire* someone when you think he or she is a good person.
closer	nearer to each other
fond	If you like someone, you're *fond* of them.
get to know	learn to know well
guilty	A *guilty* person has done something wrong
in love	When you are *in love* with someone, you want to be with them as much as possible and find them sexually exciting.
last (verb)	not stop
lucky	Someone with good luck is *lucky*.
relationship	the way in which people get on with one another
real	true
silly	the opposite of *serious*

6 Imagine you are one of the other people in the picture (Janet, Alice or Eric). You are also upset about the situation. Write a letter to the radio programme asking for help.

7 Work in groups of three or four. Prepare the radio advice programme answer to one of the letters. Don't write it down! Tell the other students, or record it for them.

8 Listen to the song. See how much you can understand, with your teacher's help.

Authority

A Government in Britain and the USA

1 Read the text without a dictionary.

HOW BRITAIN IS GOVERNED

Britain consists of four countries: England, Scotland, Wales and Northern Ireland. London, the capital, is the centre of government for the whole of Britain, but local authorities are partly responsible for education,
5 health care, roads, the police and some other things.

Laws are made by Parliament. There are two 'houses': the House of Commons and the House of Lords (which has little power). Members of the House of Commons are called MPs (Members of
10 Parliament); an MP is elected by the people from a particular area.

Parliamentary elections are held every five years or less. The leader of the majority party in Parliament becomes Prime Minister, and he or she chooses the MPs who will run the different departments of 15
government – the ministers. The Prime Minister and the most important ministers make up the Cabinet, which is the real government of the country.

There are three main political parties: the Labour Party (left-wing), the Conservative Party (right-wing), 20
and the Social Democrat-Liberal Alliance (centre).

Britain has a ceremonial Head of State, the King or Queen, who has no political power.

2 Read this entry from a dictionary. It gives several meanings for the word *authority*. Which of the meanings is the one used in the first paragraph of the text in Exercise 1? Which one do you think is used in the title of Unit 24?

respected store of knowledge or information: *We want a dictionary that will be an authoritative record of modern English* —compare DEFINITIVE — *~ly adv*
au·thor·i·ty /ɔːˈθɒrɪ̯ti, ə-‖əˈθɑ-, əˈθɔ-/ *n* **1** [U] the ability, power, or right, to control and command: *Who is in authority here?|A teacher must show his authority* **2** [C often *pl.*] a person or group with this power or right, esp. in public affairs: *The government is the highest authority in the country.|The authorities at the town hall are slow to deal with complaints* **3** [U] power to influence: *I have some authority with the young boy* **4** [U9] right or official power, esp. for some stated purpose: *What authority have you for entering this house?* **5** [C *usu. sing.*] a paper giving this right: *Here is my authority* **6** [C] a person, book, etc., whose knowledge or information is dependable, good, and respected: *He is an authority on plant diseases* **7** [C] a person, book, etc., mentioned as the place where one found certain information
au·thor·i·za·tion, -isation /ˌɔːθəraɪˈzeɪʃən‖ˌɔːθərə-/ *n* **1** [U] right or official power to do something: *I have the owner's authorization to use his house* **2** [C] a paper giving this right

(from the *Longman Dictionary of Contemporary English*)

3 All of these words come in the text in Exercise 1. There are two or more explanations with each word. Which explanation gives the meaning that the word has in the text?

country
(line 1)
1. land occupied by a nation
2. open land without buildings – the opposite of *town*

capital
(line 2)
1. (of letters) not small
2. town or city from which a country is governed
3. money used to start a business

house
(line 7)
1. building for people to live in
2. building made or used for some particular purpose
3. political assembly

power
(line 8)
1. ability to do or act
2. faculty of the body or mind
3. physical strength
4. energy
5. authority over people

member
(line 8)
1. one of a group
2. part of the body
3. part of a construction

hold
(line 12)
1. have in one's arm or hand
2. organise
3. believe

majority
(line 13)
1. greater number or part
2. legal age of adult responsibility

run
(line 15)
1. govern, organise, control
2. move quickly on foot
3. (of machines) work

cabinet
(line 17)
1. governing group
2. piece of furniture for storing things

wing
(line 20)
1. part of bird or aeroplane
2. part of building
3. part of car
4. category of political belief

head
(line 24)
1. part of body above shoulders and neck
2. leader; person at the top

4 Countable or uncountable? Look again at the dictionary entry. The first meaning of *authority* is marked *U* (uncountable); the second meaning is marked *C* (countable). Do you know what this means?

5 Are these words countable or uncountable (or both)?

1. road   education   house   power   member   difference   cabinet   water   glass   idea   money   music   piano

2. English   information   luggage   news   travel   hair   weather

6 Look at how *who* and *which* are used in the text in Exercise 1, and then complete the sentences.

1. San Fantastico, ... is the capital of Fantasia, is the centre of government.
2. The Fantasian Parliament, ... has little real power, has 300 members.
3. Our MP, ... is a woman, has a majority of 15,000.
4. Fantasia has 17 parties, ... are all very different.
5. The party .... our MP belongs to is called the New Radical Alliance.
6. The last election, ... took place five years ago, was won by the Progressive Democratic Party.
7. Cabinet ministers are the people .... really govern the country.
8. The President of Fantasia, ... is paid a very high salary, is elected for life.

7 You will hear part of a talk on the government of the United States. Before you listen, look at these notes.

US federation 50 states
48 between Canada/Mexico, + Alaska, Hawaii.
fed cap Washington, S of N Y, near E coast.

8 Now listen to the next part of the talk and try to complete these notes.

Washington centre federal govt, but each state has own...
State govts make own laws, responsible for...

9 Now listen to the rest of the talk and try to make notes yourself. (You will need abbreviations for these words: *Congress, Representatives, Senate, Democrats, Republicans*.)

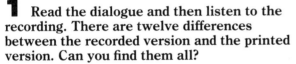

B All right, I suppose so

1 Read the dialogue and then listen to the recording. There are twelve differences between the recorded version and the printed version. Can you find them all?

TONY: Mum, can I have a party next weekend?
MOTHER: Well, I don't know. How many people?
TONY: About 20, I think.
MOTHER: You're not going to invite that Edwards boy, are you?
TONY: Well, —
MOTHER: Because I'm not having him in the house.
TONY: All right, Mum, Well, can I?
MOTHER: You remember what happened last time?
TONY: Oh, go on, Mum. We'll be very careful. I promise.
MOTHER: Well, all right, I suppose so. But you *must* tell me exactly how many are coming, and you *must* tidy up afterwards.
TONY: OK, Mum.
MOTHER: And do be careful of the carpet.
TONY: All right, Mum.
MOTHER: And you won't play your father's jazz records, will you? You know he doesn't like you to.
TONY: No, Mum, OK.
MOTHER: And you *must* get everybody out by midnight.
TONY: Yes, Mum.
MOTHER: And don't make too much noise, will you?
TONY: No, Mum.
MOTHER: And don't...

2 Try to complete this dialogue with the words and expressions from the box. Then listen to the recording and see if you were right.

afraid been trying been waiting by for goes have to have to if me to month must must to urgent us to won't you to

MR L: Er, Miss Collins.

MISS C: Yes, Mr Lewis?

MR L: I'd like .... do a couple of letters for me, ... you don't mind.

MISS C: Well, er, Mr Martin has just asked .... do a letter for him. He says it's ....

MR L: Well, I'm .... he'll .... wait. I've .... to get these letters written all week, and they .... go today. I .... keep you long.

MISS C: Right, Mr Lewis.

MR L: This letter is .... John Barlow, at Barlow and Fletcher, in Manchester.

'Dear Mr Barlow

Thank you for your letter of April 14, in which you ask .... wait a further six weeks for delivery of our order. I am afraid that this is out of the question. We have already .... eight weeks .... these urgently needed parts, and we .... have them by the end of the .... If they do not arrive .... April 30, I regret to say that we shall .... cancel the order and look elsewhere.

Yours sincerely

Paul Lewis'

See that .... today, Miss Collins, would you?

MISS C: Yes, of course, Mr Lewis.

MR L: And now a letter to...

3 Can you complete the sentences?

1. Tony's mother told him .... invite the Edwards boy.
2. She told him .... her how many were coming.
3. She .... tidy up afterwards.
4. She .... of the carpet.
5. She .... play his father's jazz records.
6. .... everybody out by midnight.
7. .... noise.
8. Mr Lewis asked Miss Collins .... a couple of letters for him.
9. Mr Barlow had .... Mr Lewis .... six more weeks.
10. Mr Lewis .... see that the letter went the same day.

4 Say these sentences in two ways: first with an ordinary pronunciation of *must* (/ms/) and then with an emphatic pronunciation (/mʌst/).

1. You must tell me.
2. You must tidy up afterwards.
3. You must get everybody out.
4. They must go today.
5. We must have them by the end of the month.

5 Look at the dialogues and write down ten or so expressions that you want to learn and remember.

6 Work with another student and prepare a conversation for one of the following situations. Use some of the expressions that you have learnt from the dialogue.

1. A fifteen-year-old asks his or her father or mother for permission to go on a cycling holiday abroad.
2. A boss asks his or her secretary to do something; the secretary has too much work.
3. A fourteen-year-old wants to go to an all-night party; father or mother doesn't like the idea.
4. A shop assistant asks the manager for a day off.

Note: For the next lesson (Unit 25 Lesson A) you may need to bring pictures. Ask your teacher.

Look and listen

A | I don't know much about art, but I know what I like

1 Listen to the first part of the recording. Which picture do you think the people are talking about?
Now listen to the second part. Which picture are they talking about?

2 Do you like any of the pictures? Which do you like best (or least)? What kind of pictures do you like?

3 Look at these sentences.

I like modern painting very much.
   (NOT ~~I like very much modern painting.~~)
I like the Hilliard picture best.
   (NOT ~~I like best...~~)
I don't like bright colours much.
   (NOT ~~I don't like much...~~)

Now put the words in order to make sentences.

1. painting much Otto Dix like the very I .
2. best snow I picture the like .
3. don't picture I this much like .
4. much the picture man don't of I like the very young .
5. I colours the Hilliard the much picture like in very .

4 Put in *very* or *too*.

1. I think Sylvia von Harden's face is .... interesting.
2. I don't like the colours in the picture of the woman; they're .... strong.
3. There are some .... amusing people in the snow picture.
4. The leaves and the clothes in the Hilliard picture are .... well painted.
5. The Avercamp picture has .... many things happening in it; it's not easy to look at.
6. A lot of modern painting is .... abstract for me; I like pictures of real things and people.

5 Match words from the two columns.

statues   composer
plays   potter
films   writer
music   actor
books   sculptor
pottery   director
pictures   painter

Can you find words ending in *-er* for the following?

a person who drives
somebody who dances
a person who climbs
a person who builds houses
somebody who looks after a garden
somebody who plays football
a person who sings
somebody who runs
somebody who cleans

6 Pronunciation. The letter *r* comes in all of these sixteen words. In standard British English, *r* is only pronounced in six of the words. Which six?

picture   potter   pottery   painter   runs
hurry   first   part   far   real   try   word
fourteen   foreign   tired   modern

Pronounce these words and expressions.

ordered   wondered   answered   preferred
remembered   covered   mattered

painter has   painter takes   painter makes
painter leaves   painter covers
painter asks   painter empties
painter isn't   painter orders
painter understands

7 Work in groups. Write ten questions ending in *by* about books, films, music, etc. Then test other students. Examples:

'Who was **The Third Man** directed by?'
'Who was **Tom Sawyer** written by?'
'Who was **Carmen** composed by?'

8 Work with three or four other students. Choose one of the statements below. You must make sure that all the other students in your group express their opinions on the statement you have chosen.

1. If a painting is really good, you don't have to be educated to like it.
2. A lot of so-called 'great art' is rubbish.
3. Too much public money is spent on art museums.
4. No individual should be able to own a great work of art.
5. The statues and other works of art that have been taken from places like Greece and Nigeria should be returned to them.
6. A great photograph can be as fine a work of art as a great painting.

B Quite a choice

Dolly Parton

1 Try to fill the blanks with words from the box. Then listen to the recording and see if you were right.

about at but don't for
let's one then

A: Where shall we go, ...?
B: How .... a concert?
A: OK. .... see what's on near here. Here we are. We've got quite a choice. Bach, Haydn and Mozart; or Stravinsky; or Ewan MacColl – he's a folk singer, isn't he?
B: Yeah.
A: Or Dolly Parton.
B: Which .... do you prefer?
A: Don't mind, really. I'm not mad about country and western, ... otherwise I'm easy.
B: What about Stravinsky, then – I haven't heard any Stravinsky .... a long time.
A: OK. It's .... eight, so we've got plenty of time.
B: Great. Why .... we have a drink somewhere first?

Now choose four or more useful words or expressions from the dialogue. Write them down.

2 Listen to the recording. You will hear three songs: *The Riddle Song, Logger Lover* and *What Did You Learn in School Today?* Copy the table and mark your reactions to each song (√ = like; ✗ = dislike; − = no opinion).

	Tune	Words	Singer
Riddle Song			
Logger Lover			
What Did You...			

Compare your reactions with another student's. Examples:

'I like *Logger Lover* best.'
'I like the tune.'
'I think the words are silly.'
'I can't stand it.'
'I don't like the singer's voice.'

Ewan MacColl

3 Work in groups. Decide on one of the three songs that you would like to hear again. Speak English! You can use some of the words and expressions from Exercise 1.

4 Listen to one of the songs again. Study the words; use a dictionary or ask questions. (The words are on pages 158–159.)

5 Grammar. Put in *which* or *what*.

1. .... of the three songs do you prefer?
2. .... sort of music do you like?
3. .... time is the concert?
4. We can listen to the record now or after dinner – .... do you prefer?
5. ....'s your favourite sort of music?
6. If you could play the piano, the violin or the trumpet, ... instrument would you choose?
7. 'Your sister came and borrowed your new record.'
   '............ sister – Liz or Judy?'

6 Match the questions and the answers. Some answers can go with more than one question.

Which guitar is yours?   Sentimental ones.
Which seats are ours?   The one by the stairs.
Which room do you practise in? The new one.
Which is your favourite song?   The biggest one.
Which record shall I put on?   The one about being lonely.
What sort of songs do you like? The ones near the front.

7 Pronunciation. Say these words.

1. guitar Mozart Parton mark start
2. your record sort four more born
3. stairs compare where there share
4. here near hear beer we're ear
5. word work world heard learn early certain hers weren't bird shirt skirt girl turn fur

8 Write down this conversation. Listen to the recording and decide where to put the question-marks (?).

1. John.
2. Peter.
3. Tired.
4. Tired.
5. Thirsty.
6. Drink.
7. Beer.
8. Music.
9. Yes.
10. Good day.
11. Terrible.
12. Problems.
13. You know Jake.
14. Jake.
15. Jake Lewis.
16. Friend of Janet's.
17. Well.
18. His wife.
19. Mary.
20. Mary.
21. Yes.
22. More beer.
23. Yes.
24. She's mad.
25. Mad.
26. Mad.
27. Listen...

Different kinds

A Animals and man

1 Do you know the names of some of these? Work in groups, and try to match as many of the words and pictures as possible.

> backbone bat dinosaur dog eagle frog
> insects shark shell skeleton snake tiger
> trout whale

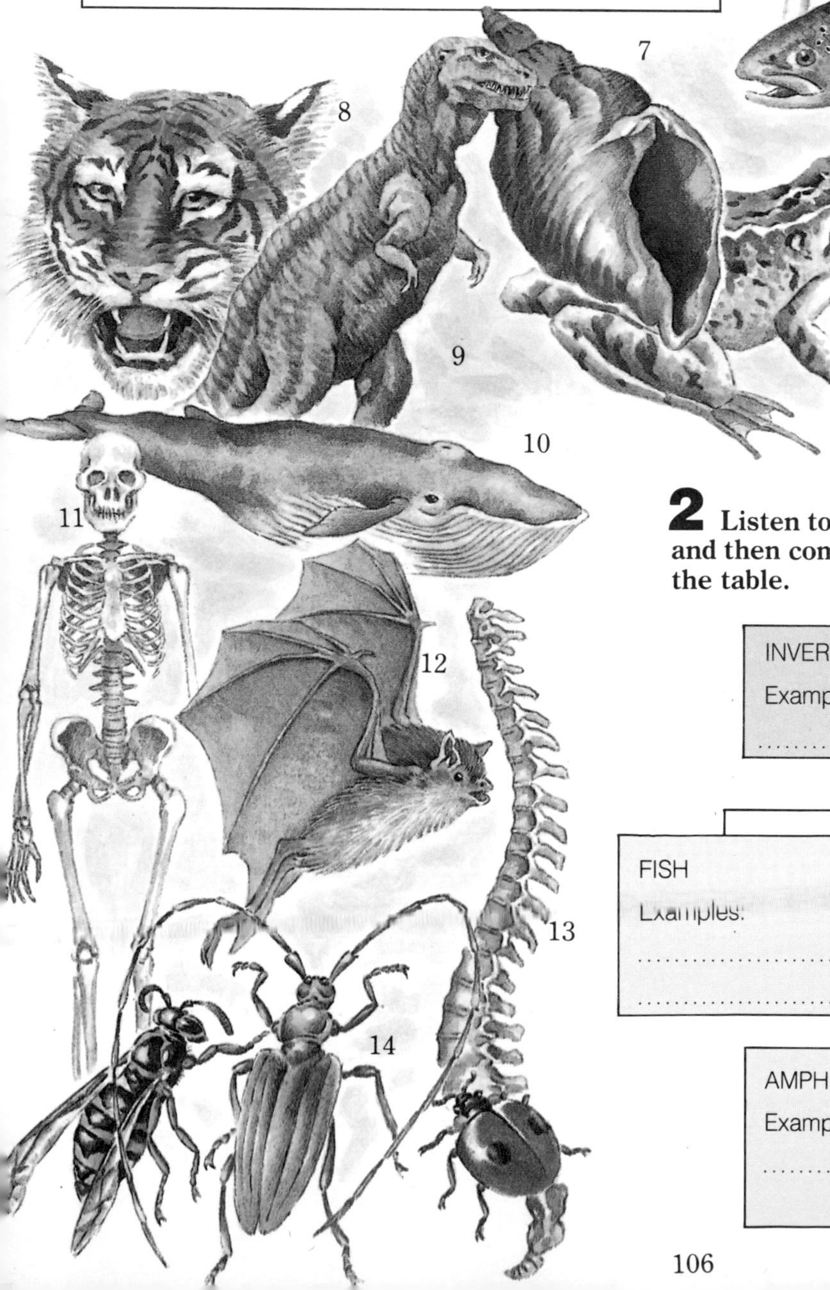

1

2

3

7

8

5

6

4

9

10

11

12

13

14

2 Listen to the talk and then complete the table.

ANIMALS

INVERTEBRATES	
Example:	

FISH	REPTILES	MAMMALS
Examples:	Example:	Examples:

AMPHIBIANS	BIRDS
Example:	Examples:

3 Complete the sentences with words and expressions from the box.

all	although	are related	be divided	belong	different
except for	for example	in many ways	kinds	main	most
only	or	others	several	typical	

1. There are two .... of bank account: current and deposit.
2. Chinese looks like Japanese, but actually the two languages are very ....
3. British and American people are like each other ....
4. Some birds – .... robins – eat insects.
5. .... bats can fly, they are not birds.
6. Dogs can .... into two kinds: those that .... to wolves and those that are more like jackals.
7. Spaghetti is a .... Italian food.
8. Not .... people who live in the United States speak English.
9. February is the .... month that has 28 days.
10. Cows .... to a group of mammals called herbivores, ... grass-eaters.
11. .... birds can fly.
12. There are .... different kinds of bicycles.
13. All European languages belong to the same family .... Finnish, Hungarian, Basque and one or two ....

4 Make sentences with *although*. Examples:

Whales look like fish, but they are mammals.
'Although whales look like fish, they are mammals.'

Bats can fly, but they are not birds.
'Although bats can fly, they are not birds.'

1. She's a famous actress, but she's very shy.
2. I understand your feelings, but I don't agree with you.
3. It was very late, but we went out.
4. I like my work, but I prefer doing nothing.
5. China, Russia, and Cuba are all communist countries, but their systems of government are very different.
6. It was raining, but we decided to go for a walk.

5 Complete four or more of these sentences and put them together to make a text. (You can change the order of the sentences, and you can make other small changes if you like.)

1. There are .... kinds of ....
2. Most of them are ...., but some are ....
3. .... look like ...., but actually they are very different.
4. .... is a typical ....
5. .... belong to a group of .... called ....
6. The difference between .... and .... is that .... is/are ...., while .... is/are ....
7. .... is/are like .... in many ways.
8. .... is/are not at all like ....
9. All .... are ...., except for ....
10. Most .... can ....
11. .... is/are like ...., because ....
12. .... is/are like ...., although ....

B It's a good one

1 Listen to the conversation. It is about one of the things in the box. Each time the conversation stops, say what you think. Examples:

'It might be a baby.'
'It could be a fridge.'
'It can't be a piano.'
'It must be a tree.'

baby	dog	canary	house	garden
flower	tree	car	statue	bookcase
piano	wardrobe	electric typewriter		
table	fridge	piece of beef		

2 Make up similar conversations in groups. See if the other students can work out what you are talking about.

3 Stress. Look at the pictures and listen to the sentences. There are some mistakes in the sentences. Can you correct them? Make sure you use the right stress. Example:

'It's ten past two.'
*'No, it isn't. It's ten past **three**.'*

4 Weak and strong forms. Some words have two pronunciations: a 'weak form' and a 'strong form'. Examples:

	WEAK FORM	STRONG FORM
must	/ms, məst/	/mʌst/
can	/kn, kən/	/kæn/
have	/(h)əv/	/hæv/
was	/w(ə)z/	/wɒz/

Which pronunciations do you think *must, can, have* and *was* have in these sentences?

1. I must go soon.
2. Oh, must you?
3. I really *must* stop smoking soon.
4. Yes, you must.
5. We must get some more milk.
6. I can swim, but not very well.
7. Yes, I can.
8. Nobody can understand what he says.
9. Where have you been?
10. What time do you have breakfast?
11. We've been talking about you.
12. Oh, have you?
13. I was late for work this morning.
14. That *was* nice – thank you very much.
15. Sally was here this afternoon.
16. Oh, was she?

5 Which one is different? Can you find a reason why one of the words in the box is different from all the others? Example:

'A cow is the only one that has horns.'
'We get milk from a cow, but not from the others.'

Try to find reasons like these for *each* of the words.

horse cat mouse camel lion cow

6 Now do the same for one of these boxes.

India China the USA France Egypt Israel

apple orange strawberry banana grape peach

fridge piano armchair car bus table

nose ear arm hand mouth foot

London Paris Copenhagen Peking Rio

7 Look at the pictures and ask for one of the things illustrated. You must not use its name (if you know it), and you must not use your hands to help you explain. The other students will try to decide which thing you are talking about.

Changes

A As time goes by

Sophia Loren

Yehudi Menuhin

1

2

3

Margaret Thatcher

4

King Juan Carlos of Spain

1 Which child became which adult? Try and match the pictures.

2 Look at the pictures below, taken a few years ago. How has each person changed? Use some expressions from the box.

gained/lost weight	gone grey/bald
got some wrinkles	grown a beard/moustache
started wearing...	let his/her hair grow
cut/dyed his/her hair	become famous
got more/less popular/serious/etc.	

3 How have you changed in the past ten years? Write two sentences on a piece of paper for the teacher to read to the class.

4 Work in groups. Choose one stage of life (childhood, adolescence, young adulthood, middle age, old age). Work together to decide on a list of advantages and disadvantages of the stage of life you have chosen.

Timber frame house

Labels: tile, paint, pipe, steps, banister, beam

5 Look at the picture with your teacher. Then listen to the recording and write down what happens to each of these: timber frame house, beams, steps, banisters, tiles, paint, pipes.

6 What might happen to these things? Use *get* in some of your answers.

1. A flower that no one waters
   It might die.
   ....
2. A car that is never put in a garage
3. A chair dropped from a second-floor window
4. Some food forgotten on a hot cooker
5. A white house in a polluted city
6. A door handle that's used hundreds of times a day
7. A plate put on a hot cooker
8. A book forgotten on the roof of a car

7 You will hear a man talking about a big change in his village. Are these sentences true (T), false (F), or does the man not say (DS)?

1. Most of the people in the village worked in the racing stables before the First World War.
2. Some of the young men from the village went into the army during the Second World War.
3. Some of the young men wanted to go to St Giles' Fair.
4. The farmer told them they couldn't go.
5. The young men agreed not to go.
6. The farmer owned houses in the village.
7. Later the young men found jobs at Blewbury.
8. The young men were happy with their new jobs.
9. After that things were the same in the village once again.

8 Class survey. Choose a question to ask the other members of the class.

1. Has your house or flat changed, or have you changed it, in any way since you first lived there? Explain.
2. Has your neighbourhood changed in any noticeable way since you first lived there? If so, in what way?
3. Is transport in your area better or worse than it was 15 years ago?
4. Is your neighbourhood prettier or uglier than it was when you first lived there? Why?
5. What do you think is the biggest change in your country since your grandparents' time?
6. Name some ways in which you think your grandparents' life was better than yours is.
7. Name some ways in which your life is better than your grandparents' was.

111

B If he'd been bad at maths,...

1 On February 6, 1944, Mark Perkins arrived in Switzerland. But if things had been different, ... Look at the diagram (the path of Mark's life is marked in grey) and complete these sentences.

1. He would have studied ... if he'd been bad at maths.
2. If he had studied literature, he'd have become a ...
3. If his parents had been well off, he ... to university.
4. If ... university, ...
5. He wouldn't have worked in a bank if his parents ... well off.
6. If the war hadn't started, he ... joined the army.

Now make some more sentences about how Mark's life would have been different if ...

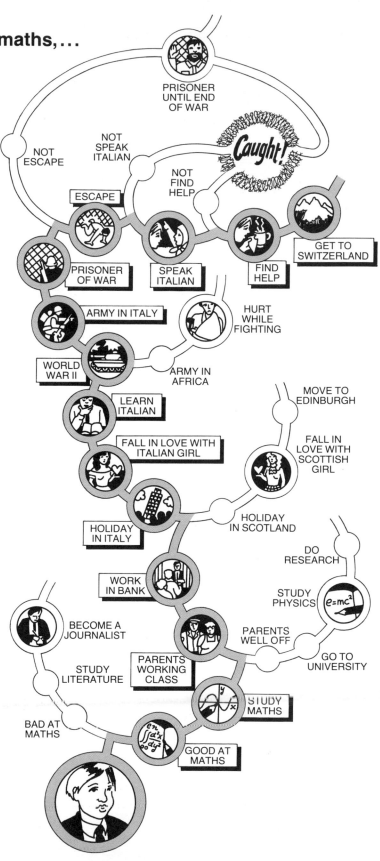

PRISONER UNTIL END OF WAR

NOT SPEAK ITALIAN

NOT ESCAPE

NOT FIND HELP

Caught!

ESCAPE

GET TO SWITZERLAND

PRISONER OF WAR

SPEAK ITALIAN

FIND HELP

ARMY IN ITALY

HURT WHILE FIGHTING

WORLD WAR II

ARMY IN AFRICA

MOVE TO EDINBURGH

LEARN ITALIAN

FALL IN LOVE WITH SCOTTISH GIRL

FALL IN LOVE WITH ITALIAN GIRL

HOLIDAY IN ITALY

HOLIDAY IN SCOTLAND

DO RESEARCH

WORK IN BANK

STUDY PHYSICS $e=mc^2$

BECOME A JOURNALIST

PARENTS WELL OFF

GO TO UNIVERSITY

STUDY LITERATURE

PARENTS WORKING CLASS

STUDY MATHS

BAD AT MATHS

GOOD AT MATHS

2 Write an *if* sentence about your own past. Then read and explain it to a few other students.

3 Put a word from the box into each blank in the text.

adopt	angry	animal	arm	car	fish	fish	hurt
local	lost	love	oil	phoned	police	put	turn

EXPENSIVE KINDNESS

A West German woman's .... for cats has brought her an .... cat and a bill for £23,000.

The story, told by German ...., began when the 56-year-old woman from Wuppertal .... her cat and .... an advertisement in the .... paper.

A man .... her to say he had found the ...., but in fact it was not hers. However, she felt sorry for the cat, which must have been a stray, and decided to .... it.

On the way home in her ...., the cat 'suddenly went wild' and bit and scratched her .... This caused the car to .... off the road and crash into a parked car, bringing down a sausage stand and a neighbouring .... and chip stand.

Boiling .... burnt the arms of a 44-year-old woman selling .... and chips, and a 21-year-old woman who was waiting for her chips fainted and .... herself falling to the pavement.

(from an article by Anna Tomforde in the *Guardian* – adapted)

4 *The woman's arm wouldn't have been burnt if the car hadn't crashed.* Make some more sentences about what wouldn't have happened.

5 Copy this list and mark the stresses in the words like this: a̰b̰o̰v̰ḛ   ins̰t̰ḛa̰d̰

1. about   advertisement   apply   material
2. conditions   society   protection   tobacco
3. besides   emergency   remember   example
4. invent   mistake   discover   impossible

What can you say about the stress in all of the words?
Now look at the first syllable of each word. Put a circle ◯ around the vowels pronounced /ə/ and a square ▢ around the vowels pronounced /ɪ/ (for example, ⓐbove; ⓘnstead). Listen to the tape or your teacher to check the answers.

6 Pronounce these words.

continue   deliver   abroad   banana   insurance
election   policewoman   repair   intelligence
Olympic   agreement   explain   disgusting

7 Work in groups. Invent the continuation of a path Mark Perkins didn't take. Then tell the rest of the class about it. Use *if.*

113

Health

A Taking regular exercise

1 Here are some things you can do to take care of your health. Which two do you think are the most important?

    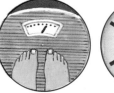

| Not smoking | Taking regular exercise | Eating good quality food | Having regular check-ups | Dieting to keep your weight down | Not drinking alcohol |

Now complete one of these sentences; write the sentence down and hand it to the teacher. The other students will try to guess which sentence is yours.

1. ... is the most important thing you can do to take care of your health because ...
2. The things I do to take care of my health are: ...
3. I think that ... is more important for your health than ... because ...

2 Read the story without a dictionary. Don't worry if you don't understand everything. Try to write titles for the pictures with blanks.

Debra Levy is a student at Oxford Polytechnic. A year ago she was extremely thin, got headaches, couldn't concentrate, forgot things. Her face was spotty; her stomach was almost always upset; she couldn't sleep. For 5 a long time, no one could help her. Her doctor used to give her sleeping pills, but each new kind only worked for a short while.

Then, after talking to a friend with similar problems, Debra began to think she might be allergic to foods and 10 chemicals. She went to see a specialist. The specialist tested her and found out that she was allergic to things she ate, breathed and touched.

Now Debra is much better. She takes medicine, but she also has to avoid some of the things that make her ill.

Things like chlorine in drinking water, fumes from cars and 15 chemicals in food all hurt her. So she has to drink bottled water, use a special air filter, and avoid tinned or packaged food. Fortunately she shares a house with other women who understand her problem, and they share the cooking and shopping for her diet. 20

Debra will finish her studies this year and begin looking for a job. But she is worried that this will be difficult. Most of the jobs that interest her are in London; but she cannot live there because of the polluted air. So learning what was causing her problems has complicated her life, but 25 she sleeps well and is healthy most of the time now.

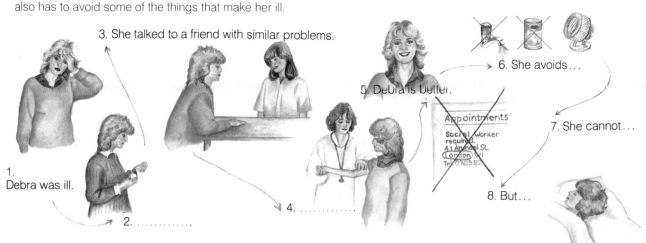

3. She talked to a friend with similar problems.

5. Debra is better.

6. She avoids...

7. She cannot...

1. Debra was ill.

2. ....

4. ....

8. But...

3 Reading skills: guessing unknown words. Match each of the words and expressions from the text (in column A) with its probable meaning in column B. The words are numbered with the lines where they come in the text.

	A	B
3	concentrate	took in through the nose
9	allergic to	think hard about one thing
10	specialist	made ill by
12	breathed	dirty
14	avoid	dirty gas caused by burning
15	fumes	made more difficult
24	polluted	stay away from
25	complicated	doctor with special knowledge

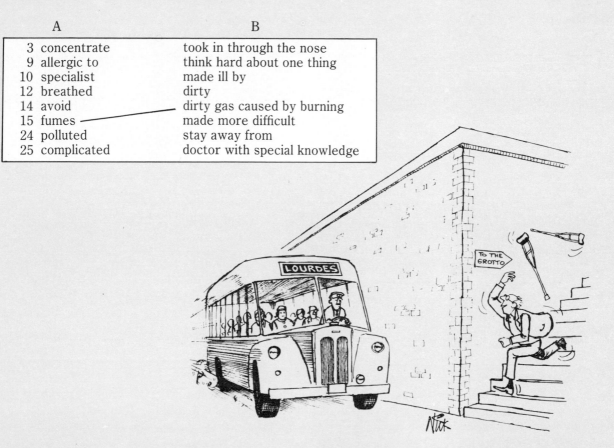

4 Look at these sentences.

She shares a house with other women who understand her problem.
She has to avoid some of the things that make her ill.
She was allergic to things she ate, breathed and touched.

Now complete the answers to these questions about the text.

1. What only worked for a short while? (The pills her...)
2. Who made Debra think she might have allergies? (A friend who...)
3. Who found out she was allergic to things she ate, breathed and touched? (The specialist who...)
4. What does she have to avoid? (The things that...)
5. Why would she like to live in London? (Because the jobs that...)

5 Think of a middle-aged person you know well (wife/husband/mother/father/friend/etc.). Imagine the doctor has told him/her to get more exercise, because of the risk of heart trouble. But he/she isn't doing anything about it. What would you do to encourage him/her? Choose two or three of the suggestions below. Add your own suggestion if you like. Then explain to other students what you would do and why.

WOULD YOU:
– buy him/her a book on exercise?
– give him/her an exercise bicycle?
– tell him/her horrible stories about middle-aged people who have heart attacks?
– ask a health club to send him/her an advertisement?
– show him/her a good example by exercising more yourself?
– promise him/her a present if he/she exercises regularly?

B Where does it hurt?

"I wish you'd called me sooner, Mrs. Moodie."

1 Read the dialogues below while you listen to the recording. Listen for the differences.

(D = doctor; P = patient)

A

D: Where does it hurt?
P: Just here, doctor.
D: Mm. And is that all the time?
P: No. Only when I walk, or when I'm going downstairs. Sometimes when I carry things.
D: When you carry things. Big things?
P: Yes.
D: I see. Now I want you to stand up...

B

D: How often do you get them?
P: Oh, three or four times a week.
D: Three or four times a week. I see. Are they very bad?
P: Oh, yes. They stop me driving. Sometimes I can hardly see, you know.
D: Yes. Do you often get colds?

C

P: It's a really bad cough. It's really bad.
D: Does it hurt when you talk?
P: If I talk a lot, yes.
D: I see. Well I'll just have a look at your chest. Do you drink?

"It's a pity you haven't got appendicitis – I'm rather good at that."

Now listen to these conversations and try to write down the words that go in the blanks.

D

P: It's a really bad pain, doctor. .... here.
D: Which side?
P: .... side.
D: How long has this been going on? When did it start?
P: .... morning, doctor. I thought perhaps it was indigestion, but it's too .... for that.
D: .... Now just .... down here. That's right. Now .... exactly does it hurt? Is it here?
P: Ooh! Yes!

E

D: Good morning, ... Palmer. What's the ....?
P: Well, I've got a .... sore throat, ...
D: .... How long have you had it?
P: Oh, about .... It's .... very painful. It's difficult to ....

F

P: It's every .... about the same time, doctor. Stuffed-up nose, my .... itch, and I feel sort of .... the whole time.
P: Is it .... when you're inside or outside?
P: When I'm in the ....

G

P: I get this .... when I bend ...., doctor. Just here.
D: I see. Take your .... off.

2 Copy this list, and then close your book. Find out what each of the words or expressions means, by using a dictionary or asking your teacher. Then listen to the conversations again. Which patient has which problem?

headaches   bronchitis   back trouble
appendicitis   a pulled muscle
hay fever   tonsilitis

3 Here are some more things the doctor said.

A Don't carry heavy things for a while.
B I think you should make an appointment at the Eye Hospital.

And here is what the patients told their families.

A He told me not to carry heavy things.
B He advised me to make an appointment at the Eye Hospital.

What do you think the doctor told the other patients? Work in groups to decide, and report to the class. You can use words from the box below, or ask your teacher for help. Begin your sentences like this:

'We think the doctor told/advised patient C . . .'

to have: an operation	some physiotherapy
some tests	a rest an injection
to take: some tablets	some medicine
some syrup	some vitamins
to wear: a bandage	
to do: some exercises	

4 Pronunciation. Say these sentences. Don't separate the words.

Where does it hurt?
Only when I run.
I want you to stand up.
How often do you get them?
They stop me working.
Sometimes I can hardly see.
Do you ever get hay fever?
It's a really bad cough.
It's a really bad pain.
This side.
Just lie down here.
It's difficult to eat.
It's every year about the same time.
I get this pain.

"All right, all right, we'll do it your way, but I still say the appendix is on the right."

5 Are you likely to have a heart attack? Work with a partner: ask each other the questions below, and note down the answers. Then your teacher will tell you how to score the questionnaire.

1. Do you usually eat very quickly?
2. Do you sometimes do more than one thing at a time – for example, boil water for your morning coffee while getting dressed?
3. Do you ever have trouble finding time to get your hair cut or styled?
4. Are you often in a hurry?
5. Is success in your work very important to you?
6. Do you get upset if you have to wait in a queue?
7. Is finishing a job you've started very important to you?

Now imagine you are working for an insurance company. Your job is to make up a questionnaire for people who want life insurance. You don't want to give insurance to anyone who is likely to die very soon!

6 Look back at the dialogues in Exercise 1 and note down five or more useful expressions to learn. Compare your list with those of the students sitting near you.

7 Work in pairs. Prepare a conversation between a doctor and a patient. Use at least two of these words or expressions in the conversation. You can ask your teacher for help with other words.

often   usually   sometimes   never
always   every year/week/etc.
two or three times a . . .   all the time
the whole time

Unit 29
Heads

A   What sort of brain have you got?

1 Listen to the recording. There are ten pieces of conversation. Which of these words goes with which piece? (There may be more than one answer.)

analysing   calculating   classifying
drawing logical conclusions   forgetting
idea   imagination   making decisions
memory   planning

2 What sort of intelligence have you got? Give yourself marks from 1 to 5 for each of the following mental abilities. (1 = very bad   2 = poor   3 = average   4 = good   5 = very good) Which of these abilities do you think are most important? Can you think of any others?

– mathematical ability
– artistic ability
– memory
– imagination
– sense of humour
– decisiveness
– planning ability

– quick thinking
– ability to analyse problems
– logical thinking
– ability to deal with large numbers of facts
– ability to learn new things
– practical common sense

3 Stress. Say these words.

analyse   **class**ify   **me**mory   **prob**lem   **log**ical
practical   **hu**mour

for**get**   i**de**a   in**tel**ligence   de**ci**sion
con**clu**sion   mathe**mat**ical   ar**tis**tic   a**bil**ity

imagi**na**tion

4 Do you wish you had a better brain? Which abilities would you like to improve? Examples:

'I wish I had more artistic ability.'
'I wish I could remember people's names.'
'I wish I was better at making decisions.'

5

Logic test. Put 'T' if the argument is a good logical one which leads to a true conclusion. Put 'F' if the argument is illogical and leads to a false conclusion.

1. I am taller than John. John is taller than Kim. Therefore I am taller than Kim. ..T..
2. My brother lives in France. People who live in France often drink wine. Therefore my brother often drinks wine. .F...
3. My secretary is not old enough to vote. My secretary has beautiful hair. Therefore my secretary is a girl under 18.
4. The person who telephoned was drunk. He had an Irish accent. He said he was an old friend of my wife's. My wife's only Irish friend doesn't drink. Therefore the person who phoned was lying.
5. All North Fantasians have blue eyes. My Fantasian friend Eric Dogwesk is good at smashball. Smashball players often eat cucumbers. All South Fantasians have green eyes. All tall strong Fantasians are good at smashball. Eric Dogwesk has green eyes and hates cucumbers. All blue-eyed Fantasians are tall and strong. All smashball players sing sentimental songs in the bath. All green-eyed Fantasians are short and fat. Therefore:
   a. Eric Dogwesk sings in the bath.
   b. Eric Dogwesk is not a North Fantasian.
   c. Eric Dogwesk is strong and tall.

6

Memory test. Turn to page 159. You will see a square with twenty words in it. Study them for exactly two minutes. Then close your book and see how many of them you can write down.

7

Are you good at organising? Study the plan and the information. Then work in groups and find a good way of reorganising the zoo.

INFORMATION
1. The giraffe is going to have a baby soon, so it must be put somewhere quiet.
2. One of the lions has died; the other should move to a smaller enclosure.
3. Small children are frightened by seeing the crocodiles as they come in.
4. The zoo has been given a new panda.
5. The monkeys are very noisy.
6. The camel is rather smelly.
7. All the enclosures should be filled.
8. Harmless animals should not be put next to predators (animals which are their natural enemies and might frighten them).
9. The zoo has enough money to buy two wolves or four flamingoes or a pair of small deer.

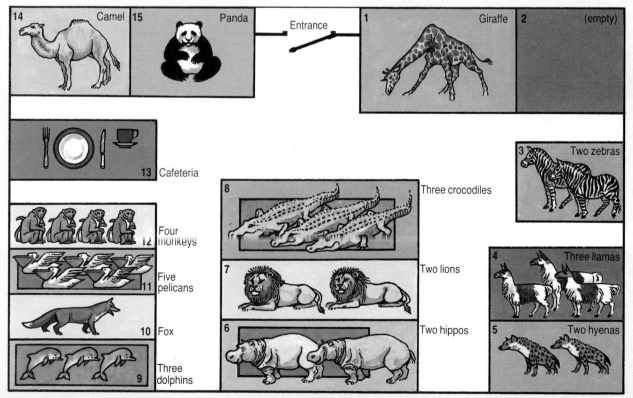

B Take your choice

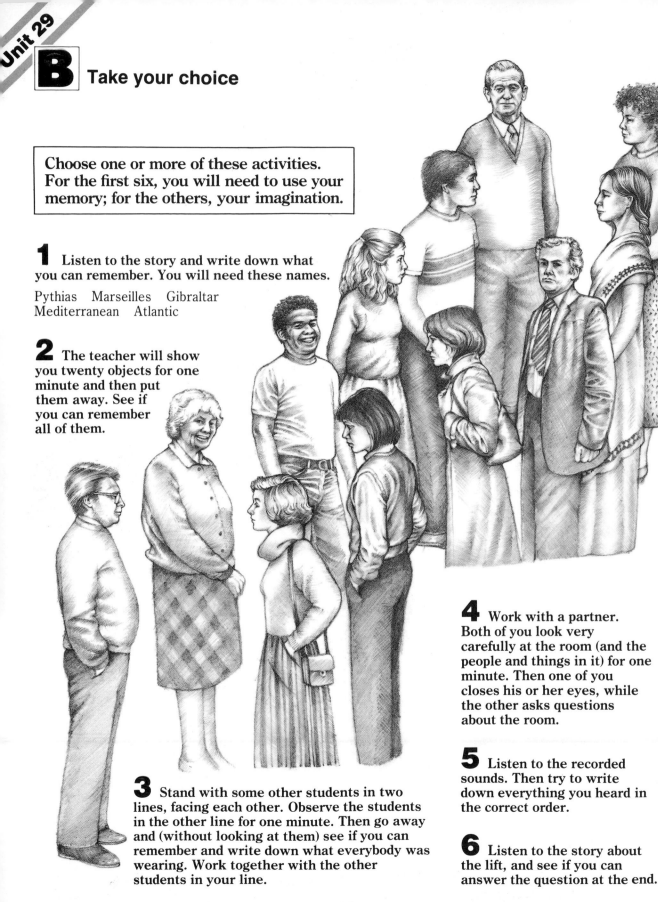

Choose one or more of these activities.
For the first six, you will need to use your
memory; for the others, your imagination.

1 Listen to the story and write down what
you can remember. You will need these names.

Pythias   Marseilles   Gibraltar
Mediterranean   Atlantic

2 The teacher will show
you twenty objects for one
minute and then put
them away. See if
you can remember
all of them.

3 Stand with some other students in two
lines, facing each other. Observe the students
in the other line for one minute. Then go away
and (without looking at them) see if you can
remember and write down what everybody was
wearing. Work together with the other
students in your line.

4 Work with a partner.
Both of you look very
carefully at the room (and the
people and things in it) for one
minute. Then one of you
closes his or her eyes, while
the other asks questions
about the room.

5 Listen to the recorded
sounds. Then try to write
down everything you heard in
the correct order.

6 Listen to the story about
the lift, and see if you can
answer the question at the end.

120

7 Mime a machine. See if the other students can write down the name of your machine.

8 Tell the class something about yourself (family, childhood, school, ...), but put in three lies. See if the other students can guess which are the lies.

9 Six of the students are travel agents. They will try to sell holidays in Greenland, Siberia, the Sahara Desert in August, Manchester in November, and similar places. The other students will go round making enquiries about holidays. See which agent does the best job of selling.

10 A rich woman has offered £10,000 to pay one person to spend a year doing as much good as possible to the world's people. Three students are the committee who have to decide who will get the prize. The other students work in groups of three or four; in each group, one student is a candidate for the prize, and the others are their families who help them prepare for the interview. After fifteen minutes' preparation, the committee interviews each candidate in turn.

11 You have just arrived in a spaceship from a distant world. You are studying the earth's civilisation, but you don't know much about it yet. The teacher will give you some everyday things: try to decide what they are for.

12 Work with some other students and prepare a modern version of a fairy story.

13 Make up a class story. One person starts, the next person continues, and so on in turn. Here is a possible beginning:

'*Mary was walking home late at night...*'

Work

A Working makes me think

In Japan, teachers earn far less than factory workers.

In Denmark, teachers are among the best-paid workers.

A New York dustman makes three times as much as an Indian army general.

A German bus driver gets twice the pay of a British bus driver.

In China, university professors earn as much as government ministers.

Chinese journalists are the worst-paid journalists in the world.

1 In your country, which of the following people are well paid? Which ones earn average wages? Which ones are badly paid? Make three lists on a piece of paper. Then try to arrange each list in order of earnings.

bus driver   company director   dustman
factory worker   farm worker   army general
government minister   nurse
primary-school teacher   housewife
university professor

2 In your opinion, which of the people in Exercise 1 should be paid most? Which should be paid least? Should any of the others be better paid, or worse paid, than they are? Compare your opinion with two other people's and report to the class.

3 Copy the list below. Then you will hear four people: John (who works with racehorses), Jane (a part-time legal secretary), Keith (a printer's reader) and Sue (a nurse). Write down what they like and dislike about their jobs.

WHO DISLIKES:
the routine of the job?
not having enough time to do the job well?
the old-fashioned way of working?

WHO LIKES:
the contact with people?
having to think?
travelling?
the job itself?

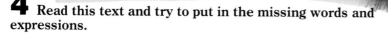

4 Read this text and try to put in the missing words and expressions.

Alan is .... commercial traveller. He works for a firm .... manufactures and sells different kinds of industrial glue. He .... most of his time travelling, visiting customers and possible customers in various .... of the country.

Alan doesn't .... his job much, and he is unhappy for several reasons. First of all, he .... living out of suitcases. When he was younger he .... the travelling, but now he is tired of .... from one hotel room to another, spending his life visiting factories in small industrial towns. And he doesn't enjoy .... with the people he meets. He gets on well enough with them, but he doesn't .... they have very much in common. Alan's interested in literature and politics. Most of the .... managers he meets just seem to be .... in talking about work and golf. Alan doesn't find glue very interesting – in fact, he would be .... if he never .... a tube of glue again in his whole life.

Although the .... and the conditions are good, and his firm treats him well, Alan would very much like to .... his job. He .... to stay in one place and see more of his .... and children. Unfortunately he doesn't have much choice; it isn't easy to find .... these days, and Alan is fortunate to be employed. Still, he can't wait to retire. He knows he is lucky in many ...., but sometimes he .... so unhappy that he wants to scream.

5 Pronouncing the letter u. Listen to the pronunciation of each group of words and try to make a rule. After you have worked out all the rules, say which group each of the words in the box belongs to.

1. bus   cut   drug   much   dustman   under
2. university   music   tune   produce   fuel   cure   communicate
3. rule   ruin   suitcase   superstition   blue   glue
4. nurse   turn   church

burglary	introduce	stupid	jump	universe	
hut	butter	fruit	suit	amused	burn
customs	use	true	computer	purpose	run

Notice these common exceptions:

put   pull   push   busy   business   truth

And of course, u is usually pronounced /ə/ when it is not in a stressed syllable, as in these words:

figure   literature
(and other words ending in -ure)
suppose   surprise   until   industry
fortunate(ly)   unfortunate(ly)

6 Which of these things do you think are most important in a job? Choose the four most important and the one least important thing. Then try to find someone else in the class who has made the same choice as you.

working with nice people   security
good holidays   good pay   short hours
getting on with your boss   travelling
comfortable working conditions   a good pension
interesting work   the chance of promotion
responsibility   freedom

7 Write one or two things you like and one or two things you don't like about your present job or activity. The teacher will read everyone's likes and dislikes to the class. Try to guess who has written what.

B Do you have to work long hours?

1 Work in pairs. One of you chooses a job from this list (without telling his or her partner).

> architect   businessman or businesswoman
> coal miner   doctor   electrician
> housewife   lorry driver   photographer
> pilot   shop assistant   teacher

The other asks the following questions, and then tries to guess his/her partner's job.

Do you have to get up early?
Do you have to get your hands dirty?
Do you have to travel?
Do you have to think a lot?
Did you have to study for a long time to
    learn the job?
Do you have to work long hours?
Do you have to handle money?
Do you work with people or alone?
Do you have to write letters?
Do you have much responsibility?

2 Listen to the recording. You will hear a person speaking on the telephone from a factory. Answer these questions.

1. Who is speaking?
   a. the managing director
   b. the managing director's secretary
   c. the accountant
   d. the sales manager
   e. the personnel manager
2. Who is he speaking to?
   a. one of the directors
   b. his wife
   c. his secretary
   d. a customer
   e. an advertising agency
   f. a journalist
3. What do they make in the factory?
   a. shoe polish
   b. typewriters
   c. knives
   d. washing machines
   e. chairs
   f. electric heaters
   g. bicycles

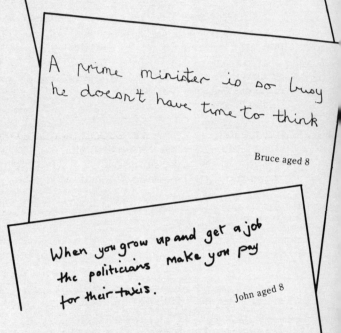

My dad works at being a striker and when I grow up I shall work there as well
George aged 6

A prime minister is so busy he doesn't have time to think
Bruce aged 8

When you grow up and get a job the politicians make you pay for their taxis.
John aged 8

3 Pronunciation of *au* and *ou*. Say these words after the recording or your teacher. Can you write the rules for *ou*?

1. /ɔ:/   automatic   cause   daughter
            fault   authority   dinosaur
2. /aʊ/   without   housewife   hours   sound
            bound   accountant
3. /ɔ:/   pour   your   four   course
4. /ə/   unconscious   previous   serious
            colour   neighbour   favour

Exceptions: aunt   laugh   draughtsman
because
should   could   would
trouble   double   couple   cousin   enough
you   through   group
although
cough
journalist

124

4 Try and fill the gaps with words and expressions from the box.

a bit	different	doing	Especially	exactly	exciting	
get on	itself	move	only	on your own	Really	
something else	sound like	terrible	working	You mean		

KATE: What do you do, ...?

PETER: I'm a mechanical engineer. Right now I'm designing a robot to .... heavy things.

KATE: That sounds .... Do you work .... or are you part of a team?

PETER: I'm the .... engineer. I should have a technician .... with me, but I don't, so I waste a lot of my time.

KATE: .... you have to go and check that they're actually building the thing the way it's supposed to be built?

PETER: Yeah. It gets .... frustrating at times. I do have a French draughtsman who works for me. He's a very good draughtsman, but not easy to .... with. Well, I don't think so, anyway.

KATE: Doesn't .... a lot of fun.

PETER: Oh, the job .... is fun. I guess there are bound to be some problems when you have a lot of .... nationalities working on the same project. .... when the other European engineers get paid much more than we do.

KATE: ....? That's ....!

PETER: I know, I know. Sometimes I think I'm mad to keep at it. But when that's what you love ...., you just can't stop and do ....

5 The teacher will give you a new job. Work with another student and prepare a 'party' conversation about your work. Try to use at least five words or expressions from Exercise 4.

Travel

A Where are they?

1 Put in the right word.

THIS
THESE
HERE
COME

THAT
THOSE
THERE
GO

1. I'd like to *come / go* away for a holiday again soon.
2. You must *come / go* and see us again one of these days.
3. Let's all *come / go* and see Harry this weekend.
4. I've found something very strange. *Come / Go* and have a look.
5. I'm afraid Mrs Barnes is busy just now. Could you *come / go* back tomorrow morning?
6. 'Newport 361428.' 'Hello, Is Helen *here / there*?' 'I'm sorry. She's not *here / there* just now.'
7. 'Moreton 71438.' 'Hello, *this / that* is Judith. Is *this / that* Phil?'
8. 'Do you know Africa?' 'No, I've never been *here / there*.'
9. '*This / That* is a nice place. I like it.'
10. 'I'm glad you like it. So do I. Have you been *here / there* before?'
11. 'No, *this / that* is my first visit.'
12. 'Have you seen *this / that*?' 'What?' 'In *this / that* morning's paper. Look!'
13. I'll never forget *this / that* morning, 20 years ago, when I first saw Mrs Newton.
14. Listen to *this / that*. You'll enjoy it. It's a great piece of music.
15. Who's *this / that* over there?
16. Jane, I'd like you to meet Peter. Peter, *this / that* is my friend Jane.
17. 'How's your lunch?' 'OK, but I don't like *these / those* potatoes much.'
18. Who were *these / those* people you were with last night?
19. Do you remember *these / those* cheese pies we used to buy in Parikia?
20. 'How do you like *these / those* trousers?' 'They really suit you.'

2 Match the words and the pictures. (There are too many words.)

tube take-off check-in taxi garage speeding bank petrol station landing delay package tour enquiry compartment waiting roundabout luxury hotel accident giving directions

3 The vowel /ə/ comes five times in these four words. Can you decide where? Where are the words stressed? Can you pronounce them?

picture   compartment   roundabout   luxury

Five of these words contain /ə/. Which ones? Can you say them?

remind   forget   afraid   minute   women
until   decide   business   comfortable   Europe

4 Look at the pictures again and listen to the pieces of conversation. Which one goes with which picture? (There is one piece too many.)

5 Listen to one of the pieces of conversation again. Try to remember exactly what was said. Can you write it down?

6 Work with another student. Prepare and practise a conversation for one of these situations (or a different one if you prefer):

– having a car repaired
– asking/giving directions
– an enquiry about air travel
– a train enquiry
– being stopped by police.

Some useful words and expressions:

CAR REPAIRS
steering   brakes   engine   plugs   starting
backfire   exhaust   silencer   tyres
puncture   windscreen wipers   wiper motor
check the brakes/steering/plugs/...
tighten the brakes/steering
change the plugs/oil/...
rust   service

GIVING DIRECTIONS
straight ahead   turn right/left at...
take the first/second on the left/right
first right, second left
keep straight on for about 500 yards
crossroads   traffic lights   fork   T-junction
you come to a T-junction

AIRPORT ENQUIRY
flight number   check-in   delay
standby   take-off   land   boarding card
smoking/non-smoking   stop over   fare
one way   round trip   hand baggage
insurance   ticket   make a reservation

TRAIN ENQUIRY
What time...?   the next train for...
Which platform...?   single   return
day return   direct   change   fast train
leave   arrive at   first class   second class
fare   ticket   seat reservation

STOPPED BY POLICE
What speed were you doing?
How fast were you going?
Is this your vehicle?
overtake   lights   traffic lights   stop sign
speed limit   speeding   driving licence
registration book
certificate of insurance
Have you been drinking?
Blow into this.

B Who has the right of way?

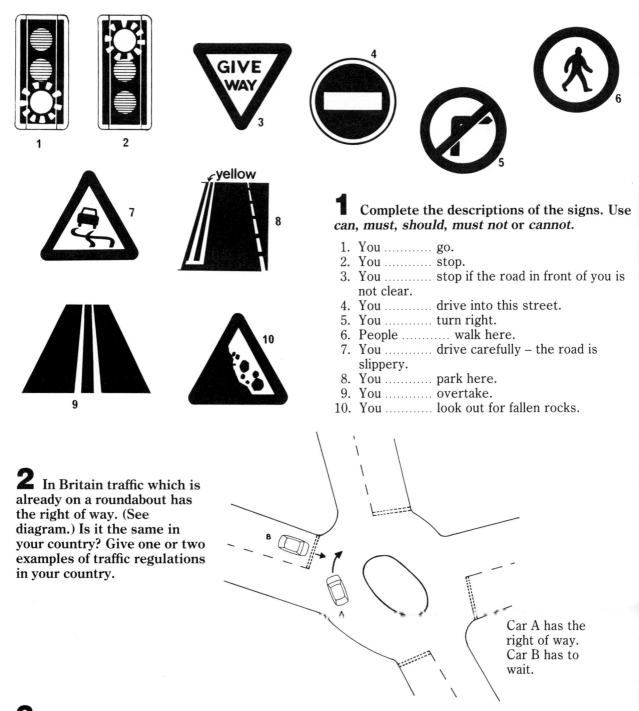

1 Complete the descriptions of the signs. Use *can*, *must*, *should*, *must not* or *cannot*.

1. You .... go.
2. You .... stop.
3. You .... stop if the road in front of you is not clear.
4. You .... drive into this street.
5. You .... turn right.
6. People .... walk here.
7. You .... drive carefully – the road is slippery.
8. You .... park here.
9. You .... overtake.
10. You .... look out for fallen rocks.

2 In Britain traffic which is already on a roundabout has the right of way. (See diagram.) Is it the same in your country? Give one or two examples of traffic regulations in your country.

Car A has the right of way. Car B has to wait.

3 Make up some traffic regulations for Fantasia (a strange country where everything is different). Example:

'You must not drive at over 30mph on Sundays.'

128

4 Read the newspaper report. Then look at the two maps and choose the map which corresponds to the report. Find on the map: a roundabout, a pedestrian crossing, a junction.

Smash girl in a tizzy

MOTORIST Lesley Aston doesn't remember much about her trip home from work.

But villagers at Studley, Warwicks, will never forget it.

First, her Austin 1300 rammed the back of another car waiting at a junction.

She drove off without stopping, overtook cars waiting at a pedestrian crossing and swung into a roundabout on the wrong side.

Then 20-year-old Lesley crashed head-on into a second car, swerved into a third and careered into a brick wall before coming to rest on a garage forecourt.

She later told police that she had only vague memories of what had happened, magistrates were told yesterday at Alchester, Warwicks. Lesley, of Hewell Road, Redditch, Worcs, was fined £150 for reckless driving and failing to stop after an accident or report it.

5 The following words spelt with *th* come in the text.

the   another   without   then   third   that

In one of the words, *th* is not pronounced the same as in the others. Which one? Can you find more words to illustrate each pronunciation of *th*?

6 Read the article again and try to guess the meaning of the following words and expressions.

trip   rammed   head-on   vague   fined
reckless   failing to stop

7 Read the following account of an accident and draw what happened.

Car A tried to overtake car B approaching a road junction. Car C, which was coming in the opposite direction, swerved to avoid car A and crashed into a tree on the corner of the junction.

8 Write an account of an accident. Read it to another student: he or she must try to draw what happened.

Revision and fluency practice

A She sounds surprised

1 Listen and say how the people sound. You can use some of the adjectives in the box. Example:

1. 'She sounds surprised.'

> afraid   amused   angry   cross   pleased
> relaxed   sad   surprised   upset   worried

2 Listen to the recording and answer the questions.

3 How many of the questions can you remember? Example:

'She asked what I was thinking about.'

4 Here are some true sentences about one person's life. Can you complete them correctly?

1. He _would have been_ happier at school if he _had been_ good at sport. (*be; be*)
2. If his French lessons at school .... more interesting, he wouldn't have studied German. (*be*)
3. If he hadn't specialised in languages, he .... mathematics. (*do*)
4. When he was 24, he was seriously ill: if he hadn't been sent to a very good hospital, he .... (*die*)
5. He wouldn't have become a teacher if he .... a particular man. (*not meet*)
6. If he hadn't met a particular woman, he .... to live abroad. (*not go*)
7. If he .... less hard, he .... himself more. (*work; enjoy*)
8. He would not have been so happy if he .... a very good family life. (*not have*)

5 Can you make some true sentences about your life, like the ones in Exercise 4?

6 Revision of tenses. Complete the sentences with the correct verb forms.

1. 'Have you got a light?' 'Sorry, I .... n't ....' (*smoke*)
2. I .... in this country since January, but I still can't speak the language very well. (*be*)
3. Yesterday evening the telephone .... three times while I .... a bath. (*ring; have*)
4. After talking to her for a few minutes, I realised that I .... her before. (*meet*)
5. 'There's the doorbell.' 'I .... it.' (*answer*)
6. 'What's the weather like?' 'It .... again.' (*rain*)
7. How long .... you .... Susan? (*know*)
8. When .... the next train .... for Liverpool? (*leave*)

7 Make some bets. You can bet about the results of arm-wrestling contests; about tomorrow's weather; about tomorrow's newspaper headlines; or about anything else you like. Examples:

'I bet you a franc I can beat you at arm-wrestling.' 'OK.'

'I bet you 2p Peter'll win.' '4p.'

'I bet you there'll be something about the strike in tomorrow's newspaper.' 'I'm not betting.'

'I bet it rains tonight.' 'How much?'

8 Look at the cartoons and talk about your reactions. Which ones do you find funny? Which ones don't make you laugh? Are there any that you can't understand? Discuss your reactions with other students.

*"Do you mind? **I** happen to be next."*

"Oh dear, I can never remember who has right of way."

"For heaven's sake, start smoking again!"

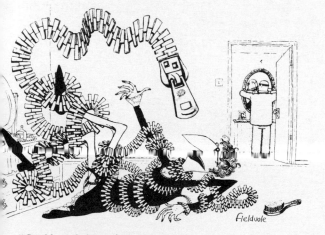

"Could you help me for a moment, Henry dear – I'm having a bit of trouble with my zip."

WHEN LIGHT FLASHES REMOVE CLOTHES

B A shock

Work in groups of four, five, or six.
Each group is to prepare, practise and perform a short sketch.
The subject of the sketch is 'a shock'.
It is up to you to decide what sort of shock this is, what you do about it, what sort of person each of you is, etc.
Besides the shock, you must also bring into your sketch at least three of the following:

– a story
– travel
– illness
– a song
– authority
– electricity
– a suggestion
– an offer
– a meal
– a bet
– money
– imagination
– something very big
– something very small

133

Unit 1: Lesson A

Grammar and structures

Introductions

Professor Andrews, this is Dr Baxter.
I'd like to introduce...
May I introduce myself?
Aren't you Henry Pollard?

'How do you do?' 'How do you do?'
I'm glad to meet you.
I've heard so much about you.
Nice to see you again.
I didn't catch your name.

Simple present tense

I work	do I work?
you work	do you work?
he/she/it works	does he/she/it work?
we work	do we work?
they work	do they work?

I do not (don't) work
you do not (don't) work
he/she/it does not (doesn't) work
we do not (don't) work
they do not (don't) work

Spelling:

he works   he stops   he starts   he likes
he wishes   he watches   he misses
he tries   he studies

Simple present tense: questions

  1   2   3
Where do you live?
  1   2   3
Where does your father live?
   (**NOT** Where does live...)

Other structures

Where are you **from**?
What nationality **are** you?
What kind of books do you like?
Can you play **the** piano?
   (**NOT** Can you play piano?)
What do you like **doing** in your spare
   time?

What does your father look **like**?
What is your mother **like**?

Asking for help in class

How do you say...?
What's the English for...?
How do you pronounce...?
How do you spell...?
What does...mean?
   (**NOT** What means...?)
Is this correct: '...'?

Words and expressions to learn

kind /kaɪnd/
spare time /'speə 'taɪm/
football match /'fʊtbɔːl 'mætʃ/
classical music /'klæsɪkl 'mjuːzɪk/
answer /'ɑːnsə(r)/
work /wɜːk/
introduce /ɪntrə'djuːs/
interest /'ɪntrəst/
travel /'trævl/
find out (found, found)
   /'faɪnd 'aʊt (faʊnd)/
go out (went, gone out)
   /'gəʊ 'aʊt (went, gɒn)/
cheerful /'tʃɪəfl/
glad /glæd/
whereabouts /weərə'baʊts/
so much /'səʊ 'mʌtʃ/

Revision vocabulary: do you know these words?

nationality /næʃə'næləti/
sport /spɔːt/
novel /'nɒvl/
flat /flæt/
first name /'fɜːst 'neɪm/
Christian name /'krɪstʃən 'neɪm/
surname /'sɜːneɪm/
Mr /'mɪstə(r)/
Mrs /'mɪsɪz/
Miss /mɪs/
Ms /mɪz, məz/

Unit 1: Lesson B

Grammar and structures

Have got

I have got (I've got)
you have got (you've got)
he/she/it has got (he's/she's/it's got)
we have got (we've got)
they have got (they've got)

have I got?
have you got?
has he/she/it got?
have we got?
have they got?

I have not (haven't) got
you have not (haven't) got
he/she/it has not (hasn't) got
we have not (haven't) got
they have not (haven't) got

We use *have got* in informal
English to talk about possession
and similar ideas, especially in the
present tense. It means the same
as *have*.

I've got a small flat in the city centre.
Have you **got** today's newspaper?
My sister **hasn't got** any children.

Be and *have*

'How old are you?' '**I'm** thirty-five.'
   (**NOT** 'I have thirty-five.')
I'm thirsty. **I'm** hungry. **I'm** hot. **I'm** cold.
What colour **is** your car?

Position of adverbs

Don't put an adverb between a
verb and its object.

I **very much** like dancing.
   OR: I like dancing **very much.**
   (**NOT** I like very much dancing.)
I **often** read thrillers.
   (**NOT** I read often thrillers.)
I **never** get headaches.
   (**NOT** I get never headaches.)
You speak English **very well.**
   (**NOT** You speak very well English.)

Like...ing

I **like** dancing.
Do you **like** cooking?

Articles

Jane is **a** secretary. (**NOT** Jane is secretar
I like dogs. (**NOT** I like the dogs.)

Words and expressions to learn

nurse /nɜːs/
secretary /ˈsekrətri/
policewoman /pəˈliːswʊmən/
T-shirt /ˈtiːʃɜːt/
ear-ring /ˈɪərɪŋ/
history /ˈhɪstəri/
newspaper /ˈnjuːspeɪpə(r)/
thriller /ˈθrɪlə(r)/
chocolate /ˈtʃɒklət/

wear (wore, worn)
 /weə(r) (wɔː(r), wɔːn)/
mend /mend/
part-time /ˈpɑːt ˈtaɪm/
slim /slɪm/
striped /straɪpt/
least /liːst/
I don't mind /aɪ ˈdəʊnt ˈmaɪnd/

Revision vocabulary: do you know these words?

clothes /kləʊðz/
shirt /ʃɜːt/
blouse /blaʊz/
sweater /ˈswetə(r)/
trousers /ˈtraʊzəz/
jeans /dʒiːnz/
skirt /skɜːt/
age /eɪdʒ/
job /dʒɒb/
height /haɪt/
daughter /ˈdɔːtə(r)/
dog /dɒg/
baby /ˈbeɪbi/

meet (met, met) /miːt (met)/
dance /dɑːns/
cook /kʊk/
shop /ʃɒp/
married /ˈmærɪd/
intelligent /ɪnˈtelɪdʒənt/
interesting /ˈɪntrəstɪŋ/
light /laɪt/
dark /dɑːk/
I can't stand /aɪ ˈkɑːnt ˈstænd/

Unit 2: Lesson A

Grammar and structures

Present progressive tense

I am (I'm) working
you are (you're) working
he/she/it is (he's/she's/it's) working
we are (we're) working
they are (they're) working

am I working?
are you working?
is he/she/it working?
are we working?
are they working?

I am (I'm) not working
you are not (aren't) working
he/she/it is not (isn't) working
we are not (aren't) working
they are not (aren't) working

We use this tense to talk about things that are happening at the moment when we are speaking or writing.

I **am going** (I'm going) down to have a word with our visitors.
It **is coming** (It's coming) down very low.
Three strange things **are getting** out.

Present progressive questions

      1   2   3
What **are** you **doing**?
      1   2   3
What **are** the President and his wife **doing**?
 (**NOT** What are doing...?)
 1   2   3
Are you **enjoying** your meal?

Spelling of -ing forms

look   looking
open   opening

come   coming } verbs ending in -e
take   taking

get   getting } verbs ending in one consonant
stop   stopping } + one stressed vowel

lie   lying } verbs ending in -ie
die   dying

Words and expressions to learn

light /laɪt/
sky /skaɪ/
machine /məˈʃiːn/
suit /suːt/
field /fiːld/
visitor /ˈvɪzɪtə(r)/
gun /gʌn/
strange /streɪndʒ/
round /raʊnd/

Revision vocabulary: do you know these words?

picture /ˈpɪktʃə(r)/
top /tɒp/
remember /rɪˈmembə(r)/
listen /ˈlɪsn/
square /skweə(r)/
across /əˈkrɒs/
inside /ɪnˈsaɪd/

Unit 2: Lesson B

Grammar and structures

The two present tenses

We use the *simple present tense* to talk about 'general time': permanent states and repeated actions.

Our light **comes** from the sun.
They usually **walk** to work.
Do you ever **drink** beer?

We use the *present progressive tense* to talk about things which are happening at or around the present moment.

The light **is coming** from a strange machine.
They **are walking** across the field.
What **are you drinking**?

Other structures

Do you **believe in** 'flying saucers'?
I **agree with** you.
I **don't agree with** you.
I **think** (**that**) you're right.

Words and expressions to learn

death /deθ/
a god /ə 'gɒd/
the future /ðə 'fju:tʃə(r)/
experience /ɪk'spɪərɪəns/
belief /bɪ'li:f/
reason /'ri:zn/
expression /ɪk'spreʃn/
nonsense /'nɒnsəns/

rubbish /'rʌbɪʃ/
guess /ges/
choose (chose, chosen) /tʃu:z (tʃəʊz, 'tʃəʊzn)/
explain /ɪk'spleɪn/
definitely (not) /'defənətli (nɒt)/
yes and no /'jes ən 'nəʊ/

Revision vocabulary: do you know these words?

life /laɪf/
dream (dreamt, dreamt) /dri:m (dremt)/
dead /ded/
sure /ʃɔ:(r)/
intelligent /ɪn'telɪdʒənt/
somewhere else /'sʌmweər 'els/

Unit 3: Lesson A

Grammar and structures

Simple past tense

I walked
you walked
he/she/it walked
etc.

did I walk?
did you walk?
did he/she/it walk?
etc.

(**NOT** ~~did I walked?~~)

I did not (didn't) walk
you did not (didn't) walk
he/she/it did not (didn't) walk
etc.

(**NOT** ~~I did not walked~~)

I went
you went
he/she/it went
etc.

did I go?
did you go?
did he/she/it go?
etc.

(**NOT** ~~did you went?~~)

I did not (didn't) go
you did not (didn't) go
he/she/it did not (didn't) go
etc.

(**NOT** ~~you didn't went~~)

The past of *be*

I was
you were
he/she/it was
we were
they were

was I?
were you?
was he/she/it?
were we?
were they?

I was not (wasn't)
you were not (weren't)
he/she/it was not (wasn't)
we were not (weren't)
they were not (weren't)

Spelling of regular past tenses

work — work**ed**
listen — listen**ed**
cook — cook**ed**
play — play**ed**

live — live**d**
love — love**d** } verbs ending in -*e*
hate — hate**d**

stop — stop**ped** } verbs ending in one vowel
fit — fit**ted** } + one consonant

marry — marr**ied** } verbs ending in consonant + -*y*
stud**y** — stud**ied**

Irregular verbs

Infinitive	Simple past	Past participle
come /kʌm/	came /keɪm/	come /kʌm/
fall /fɔ:l/	fell /fel/	fallen /'fɔ:lən/
find /faɪnd/	found /faʊnd/	found /faʊnd/
get /get/	got /gɒt/	got /gɒt/
go /gəʊ/	went /went/	gone /gɒn/
hear /hɪə(r)/	heard /hɜ:d/	heard /hɜ:d/
hit /hɪt/	hit /hɪt/	hit /hɪt/
hurt /hɜ:t/	hurt /hɜ:t/	hurt /hɜ:t/
know /nəʊ/	knew /nju:/	known /nəʊn/
learn /lɜ:n/	learnt /lɜ:nt/	learnt /lɜ:nt/
leave /li:v/	left /left/	left /left/
lie /laɪ/	lay /leɪ/	lain /leɪn/
see /si:/	saw /sɔ:/	seen /si:n/
swim /swɪm/	swam /swæm/	swum /swʌm/

Words and expressions to learn

Christmas /'krɪsməs/
Christmas Eve /'krɪsməs 'i:v/
storm /stɔ:m/
bag /bæg/
sweets /swi:ts/
bone /bəʊn/
knee /ni:/
cut /kʌt/
helicopter /'helɪkɒptə(r)/
call /kɔ:l/
hit (hit, hit) /hɪt/

stay /steɪ/
recognise /'rekəgnaɪz/
deep /di:p/
above /ə'bʌv/
afterwards /'ɑ:ftəwədz/

Revision vocabulary: do you know these words?

town /taʊn/
seat /si:t/
piece /pi:s/
plane /pleɪn/
plastic /'plæstɪk/
dress /dres/
river /'rɪvə(r)/
village /'vɪlɪdʒ/
glasses /'glɑ:sɪz/
insect /'ɪnsekt/

spend (spent, spent) /spend (spent)/
kill /kɪl/
decide /dɪ'saɪd/
die /daɪ/
arrive /ə'raɪv/
wear (wore, worn) /weə(r) (wɔ:(r), wɔ:n)/
try /traɪ/
short /ʃɔ:t/
dead /ded/
by air /baɪ 'eə(r)/

Unit 3: Lesson B

Grammar and structures

Past progressive tense

I was working you were working he/she/it was working we were working they were working	was I working? were you working? was he/she/it working? were we working? were they working?

I was not (wasn't) working
you were not (weren't) working
he/she/it was not (wasn't) working
we were not (weren't) working
they were not (weren't) working

*Just when I **was trying** to finish some work*

*Janet **turned up**.*

*I **was getting** ready to come home*

*and the phone **rang**.*

I **lost** all my money when I **was travelling from** Istanbul to Athens.
The phone rang while I **was having** a bath.

Ellipsis

(I) Had lunch with her.
(It) Sounds like a boring day.
(I) Can't remember.

Words and expressions to learn

darling /'dɑːlɪŋ/
meeting /'miːtɪŋ/
talk /tɔːk/
phone call /'fəʊn ˌkɔːl/
memory /'meməri/
turn up /'tɜːn ˌʌp/
go on (went, gone) /'gəʊ ˈɒn (went, gɒn)/
get ready /'get ˈredi/
rather /'rɑːðə(r)/

together /tə'geðə(r)/
you know /'juː ˌnəʊ/
I see /'aɪ ˈsiː/
as usual /əz ˈjuːʒuəl/
round the corner /'raʊnd ðə ˈkɔːnə(r)/
sound like /'saʊnd ˈlaɪk/
not really /'nɒt ˈrɪəli/
I can't remember /aɪ ˈkɑːnt rɪ'membə(r)/

Revision vocabulary: do you know these words?

letter /'letə(r)/
office /'ɒfɪs/
pub /pʌb/
pint /paɪnt/
journey /'dʒɜːni/
try /traɪ/
finish /'fɪnɪʃ/
ring (rang, rung) /rɪŋ (ræŋ, rʌŋ)/

Unit 4: Lesson A

Grammar and structures

Comparative and superlative adjectives

Short adjectives (one syllable) add
-er, -est.
old older oldest

Short adjectives ending in -e add -r,
-st.
late later latest

Short adjectives with one vowel
and one consonant double the
consonant.
big bigger biggest

Adjectives with two syllables
ending in -y change y to i and add
-er, -est.
happy happier happiest

Other adjectives with two or more
syllables usually add *more*, *most*.
boring **more** boring **most** boring
expensive **more** expensive
most expensive

(See diagram, Practice Book page 18.)

Irregular comparatives and superlatives

good	better	best
bad	worse	worst
much	more	most
little	less	least

Comparatives and superlatives in sentences

A car is heavier **than** a bicycle.
It has got **more** wheels than a bicycle.
  (**NOT** ...more of wheels...)
A car is not **as** fast **as** a plane.
It has not got **as many** wheels as a plane.
A car does not cost **as much** as a plane.
  (**OR:** A car costs **less** than a plane.)
It is **not nearly** as heavy as a plane.
It costs **much**/**far** more than a bicycle.
A pram is **a bit** heavier than a bicycle.

A plane is **the heaviest** of the vehicles.

Words and expressions to learn

difference /'dɪfrəns/
wheel /wiːl/
vehicle /'vɪəkl/
ship /ʃɪp/
lorry /'lɒri/
pram /præm/
horse /hɔːs/
bird /bɜːd/
piano /pi'ænəʊ/
violin /vaɪə'lɪn/
trumpet /'trʌmpɪt/
cottage /'kɒtɪdʒ/
intelligence /ɪn'telɪdʒəns/
free time /'friː ˌtaɪm/
top speed /'tɒp ˈspiːd/

Revision vocabulary: do you know these words?

tall /tɔːl/
short /ʃɔːt/
long /lɒŋ/
old /əʊld/
young /jʌŋ/
small /smɔːl/
important /ɪm'pɔːtənt/
interesting /'ɪntrəstɪŋ/
beautiful /'bjuːtɪfl/
difficult /'dɪfɪkʊlt/

Unit 4: Lesson B

Grammar and structures

The same

Her eyes are **the same** colour **as** mine.

Both

ONE-WORD VERBS
We **both speak** Chinese.
My sister and I **both like** music.

TWO-WORD VERBS
We **were both born** in September.
They **have both studied** in the USA.
Anne and Peter **can both sing** very well.

AM/ARE/IS/WAS/WERE
We **are both** fair-haired.
The two children **were both** very hungry.

Both/neither of us

Both of us like dancing.
Neither of us can swim.

Relative pronouns: who

Ann is a dark-haired woman **who** is rather shy.
Find somebody **who** speaks Chinese.

Compound adjectives

a **blue-eyed** girl
a **brown-haired** man
a **left-handed** child
a **long-sleeved** pullover

Do

She sings better than I **do.**
He likes golf, but I **don't.**

Like + -ing

I like ski**ing.**
Do you like danc**ing?**

Words and expressions to learn

fish /fɪʃ/
maths /mæθs/
company /'kʌmpəni/
director /də'rektə(r)/
pop music /'pɒp 'mjuːzɪk/
interest /'ɪntrəst/
party /'pɑːti/
computer /kəm'pjuːtə(r)/

hate /heɪt/
dark-haired /'dɑːk 'heəd/
fair-haired /'feə 'heəd/
similar /'sɪmələ(r)/
left-handed /'left 'hændɪd/
right-handed /'raɪt 'hændɪd/
broad-shouldered /'brɔːd 'ʃəʊldəd/
neither /'naɪðə(r)/
quite /kwaɪt/
I would rather not answer.
  /aɪ wʊd 'rɑːðə nɒt 'ɑːnsə/

Revision vocabulary: do you know these words?

a cold /ə 'kəʊld/
a headache /ə 'hedeɪk/
dream /driːm/
swim (swam, swum)
  /swɪm (swæm, swʌm)/
enjoy /ɪn'dʒɔɪ/
look like /'lʊk 'laɪk/
rather /'rɑːðə(r)/
shy /ʃaɪ/
alone /ə'ləʊn/
not...at all /'nɒt ət 'ɔːl/
Do you mind if...? /dju: 'maɪnd ɪf/
That's all right. /'ðæts 'ɔːl 'raɪt/

Unit 5: Lesson A

Grammar and structures

You buy meat **at a butcher's.**

a thing **with** a hole / **with** a handle
a thing / some stuff **for...ing**

Words and expressions to learn

soap /səʊp/
stamp /stæmp/
film (for a camera) /fɪlm/
tool /tuːl/
stuff /stʌf/
liquid /'lɪkwɪd/
powder /'paʊdə(r)/
material /mə'tɪərɪʊl/
hole /həʊl/
wood /wʊd/
guarantee /gærən'tiː/
make /meɪk/
cut (cut, cut) /kʌt/

deliver /dɪ'lɪvə(r)/
round /raʊnd/
Can I look round? /'kæn aɪ lʊk 'raʊnd/
I'm being served. /aɪm 'biːɪŋ 'sɜːvd/
I'm looking for... /aɪm 'lʊkɪŋ fə(r)/
That's all. /'ðæts 'ɔːl/
I'm afraid not. /aɪm ə'freɪd 'nɒt/
Anything else? /'eniθɪŋ 'els/

Unit 5: Lesson B

Grammar and structures

Infinitive with and without to

Can you **tell** me the way to...?
  (**NOT** Can you to tell me...?)
Could I **borrow** your bicycle?
  (**NOT** Could I to borrow...?)
Shall I **help** you?
  (**NOT** Shall I to help you?)
I'll **go** and get it.
  (**NOT** I'll to go...)

I would like **to go** out tonight.
  (**NOT** I would like go...)
I hope **to see** you again soon.
  (**NOT** I hope see you...)
It's nice **to see** you again.
  (**NOT** It's nice see you again.)

'Why don't you borrow something of mine?
  Would you like **to**?' 'Yes, I'd love **to**.'

Suggestions

What about your blue dress?
Why don't you borrow something of mine?

Words and expressions to learn

silk /sɪlk/
birthday party /'bɜːθdeɪ 'pɑːti/
change /tʃeɪndʒ/
iron (clothes) /'aɪən/
come round (to visit) (came, come) /'kʌm 'raʊnd (keɪm, kʌm)/
have a look /'hæv ə 'lʊk/
give somebody a hand (gave, given) /'gɪv 'sʌmbədi ə 'hænd (geɪv, 'gɪvn)/
put something back (put, put) /'pʊt 'sʌmθɪŋ 'bæk/
wait a second /'weɪt ə 'sekənd/
one of these days /'wʌn əv 'ðiːz 'deɪz/
Have you got the time? /'hæv ju: 'gɒt ðə 'taɪm/
in a hurry /ɪn ə 'hʌri/
That's very kind of you. /ðæts 'veri 'kaɪnd əv 'ju:/
I'm a stranger here myself. /aɪm ə 'streɪndʒə 'hɪə maɪ'self/

Unit 6: Lesson A

Grammar and structures

Will and *is going to*

We use *am/are/is going to* when we can already see the future in the present – when future actions are already planned, or are beginning to happen.

We're going to buy a new car.
She is going to have a baby.
It's going to rain.

We use *will* when we predict future actions by thinking, hoping or calculating.

If both parents have blue eyes, their children will have blue eyes.
I hope Ann will like these flowers.
We'll arrive in Edinburgh at about six o'clock.

May (= 'will perhaps')

If both parents are tall, their children **may** be tall too.
I **may** go to London tomorrow – I'm not sure.
    (**NOT** I may to go...)
Mary **may** come and see us next week.
    (**NOT** Mary mays...)

Words and expressions to learn

grandchild /'græntʃaɪld/
ball games /'bɔːl 'geɪmz/
science /'saɪəns/
firm /fɜːm/
(musical) instrument /'ɪnstrəmənt/
colour-blind /'kʌləblaɪnd/
sociable /'səʊʃəbl/
outgoing /'aʊtgəʊɪŋ/
optimistic /ɒptɪ'mɪstɪk/
musical /'mjuːzɪkl/
may /meɪ/
several /'sevrəl/

Revision vocabulary: do you know these words?

parents /'peərənts/
daughter /'dɔːtə(r)/
son /sʌn/
couple /'kʌpl/
baby /'beɪbi/
computer /kəm'pjuːtə(r)/
bus driver /'bʌs 'draɪvə(r)/
sport /spɔːt/
maths /mæθs/
cheerful /'tʃɪəfʊl/
shy /ʃaɪ/
depressed /dɪ'prest/
certainly /'sɜːtənli/
probably /'prɒbəbli/
what...like? /'wɒt 'laɪk/
the future /ðə 'fjuːtʃə(r)/

Unit 6: Lesson B

Grammar and structures

Present progressive with future meaning

(Used to talk about future actions which are already planned or arranged, especially when we give the time or date.)

My mother's coming down on Thursday.
    (**NOT** My mother comes down on Thursday.)
I'm going to Cardiff on Wednesday.
    (**NOT** I go to Cardiff on Wednesday.)
I'm playing tennis until a quarter past four.

Prepositions of time

at two o'clock
in the afternoon
on Tuesday
on June 17th
I'm playing tennis **until** a quarter past.
I'll ring you back **in** half an hour.
What time does the film start?
    (**NOT USUALLY** 'At what time...')

Suggestions

How about Thursday?
Shall we say Monday morning?

Would like + infinitive

I'd like to make an appointment...
I'd like you to meet my mother.
    (**NOT** I'd like that you meet...)

Take (time)

It'll take a couple of hours at least.
It'll take me a few minutes to shower and get dressed.

This and *that*

'Who's **that**?' '**This** is Audrey.'

Other structures

I wondered if you were free on Thursday.
I thought you said Tuesday.
Could we make it later?
I'll ring you back.

Words and expressions to learn

couple /'kʌpl/
shower /'ʃaʊə(r)/
diary /'daɪəri/
church /tʃɜːtʃ/
cake /keɪk/
wonder /'wʌndə(r)/
fix /fɪks/
manage /'mænɪdʒ/
practise /'præktɪs/
get changed /'get 'tʃeɪndʒd/
confirm /kən'fɜːm/
It depends. /ɪt dɪ'pendz/
Let me see. /'let mi: 'si:/
I'll ring/call you back.
    /aɪl 'rɪŋ/'kɔːl ju: 'bæk/
say,... /seɪ/
not... either /'nɒt 'aɪðə(r)/
my place /'maɪ 'pleɪs/

Revision vocabulary: do you know these words?

appointment /ə'pɔɪntmənt/
sweater /'swetə(r)/
ironing /'aɪənɪŋ/
mend /mend/
clean /kliːn/
try /traɪ/
free /friː/
early /'ɜːli/
difficult /'dɪfɪkʊlt/
I'm afraid (= 'I'm sorry') /aɪm ə'freɪd/

139

Unit 7: Lesson A

Grammar and structures

Present perfect tense

I have (I've) broken
you have (you've) broken
he/she/it has ('s) broken
we have (we've) broken
they have (they've) broken

have I broken?
have you broken?
has he/she/it broken?
have we broken?
have they broken?

I have not (haven't) broken
you have not (haven't) broken
he/she/it has not (hasn't) broken
we have not (haven't) broken
they have not (haven't) broken

We use this tense to talk about finished actions, when we are talking about an *unfinished* time period:

Have you **ever** eaten octopus?
I have **often** dreamt of being rich.
During the last three years, I have travelled 100,000 miles.

We do not use the present perfect tense when we talk about a *finished* time period.

When I was a child, I **hated** maths.
   (**NOT** ~~When I was a child, I have hated maths.~~)
I **saw** John **yesterday**.
   (**NOT** ~~I have seen John yesterday.~~)

Present perfect, simple past and simple present

Have you ever...?

PAST ------------ NOW ------------ FUTURE

Did you ever...?   *Do you ever...?*

Have you ever eaten octopus?
When you were a child, **did you ever dream** of being someone else?
Do you ever go out by yourself?

Been (past participle of *go*)

Have you ever **been** to Canada?
I've **been** to Hong Kong twice this year.

Go...ing

Do you ever **go walking** in the rain?
When you were a child, did you ever **go camping**?

Words and expressions to learn

song /sɒŋ/
job /dʒɒb/
ankle /'æŋkl/
billion /'bɪljən/
boat /bəʊt/
dollar /'dɒlə(r)/
grammar /'græmə(r)/
ice-cream /'aɪs 'kri:m/
advertisement /əd'vɜ:tɪsmənt/
climb /klaɪm/
go camping (went, gone)
   /'gəʊ 'kæmpɪŋ (went, gɒn)/
run away (ran, run)
   /'rʌn ə'weɪ (ræn, rʌn)/
fight (fought, fought) /faɪt (fɔ:t)/
past (adjective) /pɑ:st/
in hospital /ɪn 'hɒspɪtl/
recently /'ri:səntli/
on one occasion /ɒn 'wʌn ə'keɪʒn/

Unit 7: Lesson B

Grammar and structures

Present perfect for news

Police **have arrested** a man in connection with the murder of Professor Bosk.
President Martin **has arrived** for a state visit.
The Minister for Consumer Affairs **has just announced**...
Listen! Something terrible **has just happened**!

Present perfect for changes

The population **has doubled** since 1900.
There used to be two bridges, but one **has fallen** down.

Present perfect progressive

I have been working
you have been working
he/she/it has been working
we have been working
they have been working

have I been working?
have you been working?
etc.

I have not been working
you have not been working
etc.

PAST ----|----|----|---- NOW_____FUTURE

It **has been raining** for four weeks.

I **have been working** all day.
How long **have you been studying** English?
She **has been talking** on the phone since ten o'clock.
   (**NOT** ~~She is talking...since ten o'clock.~~)

Non-progressive verbs

I've **known** her for six weeks.
   (**NOT** ~~I've been knowing her for six weeks.~~)
   (**NOT** ~~I know her for six weeks.~~)
How long **have you had** that car?
She's **been** in America for three months.

140

Since and *for*

I've been here **since April.**
I've been here **for four months.**
(NOT ~~... since four months.~~)
They've been talking **since nine o'clock.**
They've been talking **for three hours.**

Used to

I **used to** play tennis a lot, but now I play football.
(NOT ~~... now I use to play football.~~)
I **didn't use to** like classical music.
Did you **use to** play with dolls when you were small?

Pronunciation: / 'juːst tə/
(NOT ~~/'juːzd tə/~~)

Words and expressions to learn

election /ɪ'lekʃən/
economy /ɪ'kɒnəmi/
president /'prezɪdənt/
trip /trɪp/
percentage /pə'sentɪdʒ/
unemployment /ʌnɪm'plɔɪmənt/
figures /'fɪgəz/
minister /'mɪnɪstə(r)/
crops /krɒps/
fruit /fruːt/
silver /'sɪlvə(r)/
increase /ɪn'kriːs/
sign /saɪn/
improve /ɪm'pruːv/
average /'ævrɪdʒ/
abroad /ə'brɔːd/

Revision vocabulary: do you know these words?

vegetable /'vedʒtəbl/
price /praɪs/
population /pɒpjə'leɪʃn/
rise (rose, risen) /raɪz (rəʊz, rɪzn)/
fall (fell, fallen) /fɔːl (fel, fɔːlən)/
win (won, won) /wɪn (wʌn)/
rain /reɪn/

Unit 8: Lesson A

Grammar and structures

Can for possibility

You **can** (/kn/) get free medical care.
(NOT ~~You can to get...~~)
Where **can** you get a good inexpensive meal?

Will and *may*

Information centres **will** have information about 'bed and breakfast'.
If 'bed and breakfast' is too expensive, there **may** be a youth hostel nearby.

Connectors

In towns and cities there are buses, **and** in London there is...
Fast food shops are cheap, **but** the food is not always very good.
The underground is not easy to use, **so** you should learn about it before you use it.
Your country may have an agreement with Britain for other medical care, **too;**...
There are **also** coaches between some towns and cities; **these** are cheaper than trains.
...a post office. Often **it** is inside a small shop.
People sometimes say 'p' instead of 'pence';
for example, 'eighty p'.

Words and expressions to learn

campsite /'kæmpsaɪt/
fare /feə/
coach /kəʊtʃ/
distance /'dɪstəns/
underground /'ʌndəgraʊnd/
accident /'æksɪdənt/
embassy /'embəsi/
consulate /'kɒnsəlɒt/
agreement /ə'griːmənt/
insurance /ɪn'ʃɔːrəns/
foreign /'fɒrən/
at least /ət 'liːst/
free /friː/
for example /fər ɪg'zɑːmpl/
also /'ɔːlsəʊ/

Revision vocabulary: do you know these words?

pence /pens/
pound /paʊnd/
hotel /həʊ'tel/
youth hostel /'juːθ 'hɒstl/
train /treɪn/

bus /bʌs/
family /'fæməli/
only /'əʊnli/
post office /'pəʊst 'ɒfɪs/
stamp /stæmp/
village /'vɪlɪdʒ/
town /taʊn/
shop /ʃɒp/
restaurant /'restrənt/
food /fuːd/
meal /miːl/
pub /pʌb/
country /'kʌntri/
journey /'dʒɜːni/
health /helθ/
change (verb) /tʃeɪndʒ/
stay /steɪ/
help /help/
buy (bought, bought) /baɪ (bɔːt)/
need /niːd/
sometimes /'sʌmtaɪmz/
usually /'juːʒəli/
often /'ɒfn/
always /'ɔːlweɪz/
cheap /tʃiːp/
expensive /ɪk'spensɪv/

Unit 8: Lesson B

Grammar and structures

Should and *will have to*

You **should take** sunglasses.
(NOT ~~You should to take...~~)
You'll **have to** have a visa.

Words and expressions to learn

operator /'ɒpəreɪtə(r)/
airline /'eəlaɪn/
wallet /'wɒlɪt/
passport /'pɑːspɔːt/
customs /'kʌstəmz/
pickpocket /'pɪkpɒkɪt/
competition /kɒmpə'tɪʃn/
choice /tʃɔɪs/
pick up /'pɪk 'ʌp/
cancel /'kænsl/
go through customs (went, gone) /'gəʊ 'θruː 'kʌstəmz (went, gɒn)/
reverse-charge call /rɪ'vɜːs 'tʃɑːdʒ 'kɔːl/
collect call (American) /kə'lekt 'kɔːl/

STD code /'es 'tiː 'diː 'kəʊd/
area code (American) /'eərɪə 'kəʊd/
immigration control /ɪmɪ'greɪʃn kən'trəʊl/

Revision vocabulary: do you know these words?

likely /'laɪkli/
easy /'iːzi/
light /laɪt/
exciting /ɪk'saɪtɪŋ/
tired /'taɪəd/
beautiful /'bjuːtɪfl/
sunny /'sʌni/
comfortable /'kʌmftəbl/

Unit 9: Lesson A

Grammar and structures

Present perfect and simple past

The present perfect tense is used to tell people about very recent past events which are 'news'. If you find a box of chocolates on your desk you can say:

Someone **has left** me a box of chocolates!
(**NOT** Someone left me...)

The simple past is used to talk about past events which are completely finished, and which are not 'news'. Compare:

My son **has** just **fallen** off a wall. I think he **has broken** his leg.
When I was ten, I **fell** off a wall and **broke** my leg.

Remember: we do not use the present perfect with 'finished-time' words.

Some of the demonstrators **left** home shortly after midnight last night.
(NOT ...have left home shortly after midnight...)

There has been

There's been an accident.

Words and expressions to learn

fire /'faɪə(r)/
neighbour /'neɪbə(r)/
kitchen /'kɪtʃɪn/
burglary /'bɜːgləri/
smoke /sməʊk/
window /'wɪndəʊ/
instructions /ɪn'strʌkʃənz/
ambulance /'æmbjʊləns/
emergency /ɪ'mɜːdʒənsi/
bleed (bled, bled) /bliːd (bled)/

steal (stole, stolen) /stiːl
(stəʊl, 'stəʊlən)/
cover /'kʌvə(r)/

Unit 9: Lesson B

Grammar and structures

Make + object + adjective
Chocolate **makes you fat.**

Make + object + infinitive without *to*
Rain **makes the flowers grow.**
(**NOT** ...makes the flowers to grow.)

Making apologies
I'm sorry. I didn't mean to do it.
I didn't mean to.
I was thinking about something else.
I forgot what I was doing.
It was an accident.
I didn't do it on purpose.

Accepting apologies
That's all right.
It doesn't matter.
It wasn't your fault.

Words and expressions to learn
cough /kɒf/
switch /swɪtʃ/
brake /breɪk/
kiss /kɪs/
mean (meant, meant) /miːn (ment)/
see (saw, seen) (= understand)
/siː (sɔː, siːn)/
burn (burnt, burnt) /bɜːn (bɜːnt)/
It doesn't matter. /ɪt 'dʌznt 'mætə(r)/
That's all right. /'ðæts 'ɔːl 'raɪt/
my/your fault /'maɪ/'jɔː 'fɔːlt/
on purpose /ɒn 'pɜːpəs/
than usual /ðən 'juːʒuːʊl/

Learn two or more of these:
accelerator /ək'seləreɪtə(r)/
row /raʊ/
control /kən'trəʊl/
sigh /saɪ/

Revision vocabulary: do you know these words?
rain /reɪn/
chocolate /'tʃɒklət/
forget (forgot, forgotten)
/fə'get (fə'gɒt, fə'gɒtn)/
jump /dʒʌmp/
get (got, got) /get (gɒt)/
crash /kræʃ/
lorry /'lɒri/
careful /'keəfl/
else /els/
actually /'æktʃəli/
because /bɪ'kɒz/
so /səʊ/

Unit 10: Lesson A

Grammar and structures

If
If you are travelling at 80kph in a car, you can stop safely in 52m.
If your ancestors' language was Choctaw, they lived in America.
If today is your golden wedding anniversary, you have been married for 50 years.

Special case: *if* + present for future idea
If you **see** a black cat you'**ll have** good luck.
(**NOT** If you will see...)
What **will happen if** John **speaks** to the girl?
(**NOT** if John will speak...)

If and *when*
When I go to bed tonight, I'll...
(I *will* go to bed.)
If I go to Scotland, I'll...
(I *may* go to Scotland.)

Negative imperatives; imperatives with *if*
Don't look at the teacher.
If today is Tuesday, **write** the number 12. **If not, don't write** anything.

Words and expressions to learn

score /skɔː(r)/
wedding /'wedɪŋ/
great-grandparents
  /'greɪt 'grænpeərənts/
century /'sentʃəri/
island /'aɪlənd/
superstition /suːpə'stɪʃn/
luck /lʌk/

shoulder /'ʃəʊldə(r)/
hat /hæt/
New Year /'njuː 'jɪə(r)/
spill (spilt, spilt) /spɪl (spɪlt)/
itch /ɪtʃ/
close /kləʊz/
drunk /drʌŋk/
safely /'seɪfli/

Revision vocabulary: do you know these words?

language /'læŋgwɪdʒ/
cat /kæt/
wine /waɪn/
salt /sɔːlt/
umbrella /ʌm'brelə/
mirror /'mɪrə(r)/
travel /'trævl/

throw (threw, thrown)
  /θrəʊ (θruː, θrəʊn)/
open /'əʊpn/
break (broke, broken)
  /breɪk (brəʊk, 'brəʊkn)/
hit (hit, hit) /hɪt/
dark /dɑːk/

Unit 10: Lesson B

Grammar and structures

Present tense with future meaning

When you **do** this, the cat will run.
  (NOT ~~When you will do this, . . .~~)
As soon as the kettle **is** full, move the fish.
Turn the small wheel **until** the kettle **is** under the tap.

When and until

When a melon is ready to eat, the end opposite the
  stem will be fairly soft.
Onions won't make you cry **until** they lose their roots.

Remember: *until* can also be used with days, dates, times, etc.

She'll be there **until** half past six.

Words and expressions to learn

tap /tæp/
tin /tɪn/
fridge /frɪdʒ/
knife (knives) /naɪf (naɪvz)/
butter /'bʌtə(r)/
onion /'ʌnjən/
turn on/off /'tɜːn 'ɒn/'ɒf/

fill /fɪl/
cry /kraɪ/
full /fʊl/
sharp /ʃɑːp/
hard /hɑːd/
last /lɑːst/

Learn three or more of these:

kettle /'ketl/
string /strɪŋ/
hook /hʊk/
bell /bel/
stem /stem/
root /ruːt/
skin /skɪn/
needle /'niːdl/

peel /piːl/
pour /pɔː(r)/
spring /sprɪŋ/
tap (verb) /tæp/
bubble /'bʌbl/
shrink (shrank, shrunk)
  /ʃrɪŋk (ʃræŋk, ʃrʌŋk)/

THERE IS NO SUMMARY FOR UNIT 11, LESSON A

Unit 11: Lesson B

Words and expressions to learn

experience /ɪks'pɪərɪəns/
salary /'sæləri/
interview /'ɪntəvjuː/
canteen /kæn'tiːn/
conditions /kən'dɪʃənz/

Managing Director /'mænɪdʒɪŋ də'rektə(r)/
qualifications /kwɒlɪfɪ'keɪʃənz/
advertise /'ædvətaɪz/
apply /ə'plaɪ/
essential /ɪ'senʃul/

full-time /'fʊl 'taɪm/
Yours faithfully /'jɔːz 'feɪθfuli/
Yours sincerely /'jɔːz sɪn'sɪəli/
look forward /'lʊk 'fɔːwəd/
I look forward to hearing from you.
as soon as possible /əz 'suːn əz 'pɒsəbl/

Unit 12: Lesson A

Grammar and structures

Simple present passive

Trees **are transported** to paper mills
by land or water.
(= Somebody transports trees to
paper mills . . .)

Made from and made into

Paper **is made from** wood. Wood **is
made into** paper.

No *the* in generalisations

Paper was invented by the Chinese.
Oil is produced in Texas.
  (NOT ~~The oil is produced . . .~~)

Words and expressions to learn

industry /'ɪndəstri/
page /peɪdʒ/
adult /'ædʌlt/
dry /draɪ/
use /juːz/
grow (grew, grown)
  /grəʊ, gruː, grəʊn)/
reach /riːtʃ/
get to /'get tə/
AD /eɪ 'diː/
by land /baɪ 'lænd/
daily /'deɪli/
serious /'sɪərɪəs/
Muslim /'mʌzlɪm/

Learn five or more of these:
rice /raɪs/
oil /ɔɪl/
coal /kəʊl/
wheat /wiːt/
wool /wʊl/
gold /gəʊld/
chemicals /'kemɪklz/
iron /'aɪən/
steel /stiːl/
plastic /'plæstɪk/
leather /'leðə(r)/
cotton /'kɒtn/
synthetic fibre /sɪn'θetɪk 'faɪbə(r)/
produce (verb) /prə'djuːs/
mine /maɪn/
manufacture /mænjʊ'fæktʃə(r)/
invent /ɪn'vent/

Unit 12: Lesson B

Grammar and structures

Simple past passive

All three **were arrested** the next morning.
The *Communist Manifesto* **was written** by
Marx and Engels.
  (NOT ⎯ *was writing by...*)

With and *by*

He was killed **with** a revolver.
  (= Someone used a revolver to kill him.)
The police think he was killed **by** his wife.
  (= The police think his wife killed him.)
His leg was broken **by** the fall.
  (NOT ⎯ *with the fall...*)

Words and expressions to learn

stone /stəʊn/
dance /dɑ:ns/
body (= dead person) /'bɒdi/
thief /θi:f/
business /'bɪznɪs/
invent /ɪn'vent/
direct /dɪ'rekt/
arrest /ə'rest/
sack /sæk/
owe /əʊ/
search /sɜ:tʃ/
import /'ɪmpɔ:t/
export /'ekspɔ:t/
alive /ə'laɪv/
central /'sentrəl/
earlier /'ɜ:lɪə(r)/

Revision vocabulary: do you know these words?

pocket /'pɒkɪt/
cash /kæʃ/
hotel /həʊ'tel/
flat /flæt/
discover /dɪs'kʌvə(r)/
kill /kɪl/
build (built, built) /bɪld (bɪlt)/
win (won, won) /wɪn (wʌn)/
dead /ded/

Unit 13: Lesson A

Words and expressions to learn

hill /hɪl/
valley /'væli/
stream /stri:m/
waterfall /'wɔ:təfɔ:l/
wood /wʊd/
path /pɑ:θ/
lake /leɪk/
town hall /'taʊn 'hɔ:l/
college /'kɒlɪdʒ/
park /pɑ:k/
central heating /'sentrəl 'hi:tɪŋ/

through /θru:/
straight ahead /'streɪt ə'hed/

Revision vocabulary: do you know these words?

across /ə'krɒs/
along /ə'lɒŋ/
up /ʌp/
down /daʊn/
north /nɔ:θ/
south /saʊθ/
west /west/
east /i:st/
mountain /'maʊntɪn/
island /'aɪlənd/

river /'rɪvə(r)/
bridge /brɪdʒ/
road /rəʊd/
town /taʊn/
car park /'kɑ: 'pɑ:k/
post office /'pəʊst 'ɒfɪs/
crossroads /'krɒsrəʊdz/
theatre /'θɪətə(r)/
cinema /'sɪnəmə/
street /stri:t/

Unit 13: Lesson B

Grammar and structures

Linking verbs with adjectives

It **looks heavy**.
  (NOT It looks heavily.)
It **is heavy**.
It **feels cold**.
It **smells funny**.

Look like, sound like etc.

Your sister **looks like** you.
It **sounds like** a train.

That: relative pronoun

a thing **that** tells you the time
an animal **that** has a very long neck

a thing (that) you sit on
something (that) you read

Prepositions at the end of relative clauses

a thing (that) you sit **on**
a thing (that) you open the door **with**
a thing (that) you drink **out of**

With

an animal **with** a long neck
  (=an animal **that has** a long neck)

You (=*people*)

A watch tells **you** the time.
A key is a thing that **you** open the door with.

Words and expressions to learn

back /bæk/
ice /aɪs/
tongue /tʌŋ/
envelope /'envələʊp/
feel (felt, felt) /fi:l (felt)/
smell (smelt, smelt)
  /smel (smelt)/
funny (=strange) /'fʌni/

Learn seven or more of these:
lid /lɪd/
calendar /'kælɪndə(r)/
suitcase /'su:tkeɪs/
hairbrush /'heəbrʌʃ/
pillow /'pɪləʊ/
sheet /ʃi:t/
wrist /rɪst/
queue /kju:/
sandwich /'sænwɪdʒ/
microphone /'maɪkrəfəʊn/
lipstick /'lɪpstɪk/
magazine /mægə'zi:n/
nail /neɪl/
overcoat /'əʊvəkəʊt/
rose /rəʊz/
umbrella /ʌm'brelə/
beer /bɪə(r)/
litre /'li:tə(r)/
oil /ɔɪl/
pig /pɪg/

Revision vocabulary: do you know these words?

top /tɒp/
boat /bəʊt/
gun /gʌn/
ice-cream /'aɪs 'kri:m/
tap /tæp/
church /tʃɜ:tʃ/
suit /su:t/
bicycle /'baɪsɪkl/
pint /paɪnt/
sweater /'swetə(r)/
cat /kæt/
sure /ʃɔ:(r)/
heavy /'hevi/
pick up /'pɪk 'ʌp/
wear (wore, worn)
  /weə(r) (wɔ:(r), wɔ:n)/
liquid /'lɪkwɪd/
alive /ə'laɪv/
useful /'ju:sfʊl/
a bit /ə 'bɪt/

Unit 14: Lesson A

Grammar and structures

Would rather

Would you **rather** live in the same town as your parents or not?
  (**NOT** ~~Would you rather to live...~~)
I'd rather take my mother on holiday with me.
I'd rather not invite my in-laws to spend a week with us.
Most people **would rather** spend less time working.

Connectors

Kim and May are married, **but** they do not want to have children.
Although they enjoy playing with their nieces and nephews, they do not want to be full-time parents.
There are a lot of couples with young children in their neighbourhood, **so** they often help one another out.
Besides her husband and her children, she **also** shares her home with her mother-in-law, . . .
Because Jack is too ill to live alone, he lives with his son Barry.
Barry is getting married soon, **and** Jack will continue to live with the young couple.

Words and expressions to learn

relative /'relətɪv/
aunt /ɑ:nt/
uncle /'ʌŋkl/
niece /ni:s/
nephew /'nefju:/
cousin /'kʌzn/
grandmother /'grænmʌðə(r)/
grandfather /'grænfɑ:ðə(r)/
granddaughter /'grændɔ:tə(r)/
grandson /'grænsʌn/
mother-in-law /'mʌðərɪnlɔ:/
father-in-law /'fɑ:ðərɪnlɔ:/
brother-in-law /'brʌðərɪnlɔ:/
sister-in-law /'sɪstərɪnlɔ:/
parents-in-law /'peərəntsɪnlɔ:/
in-laws /'ɪnlɔ:z/
society /sə'saɪəti/
rule /ru:l/
adopt /ə'dɒpt/
continue /kən'tɪnju:/
universal /ju:nɪ'vɜ:sl/
healthy /'helθi/
proud (of) /praʊd (əv)/
although /ɔ:l'ðəʊ/
besides /bɪ'saɪdz/

Revision vocabulary: do you know these words?

parent /'peərənt/
child (*plural* children) /tʃaɪld ('tʃɪldrən)/
grandparent /'grænpeərənt/
grandchild /'græntʃaɪld/
husband /'hʌzbənd/
wife (*plural* wives) /waɪf (waɪvz)/
daughter /'dɔ:tə(r)/
son /sʌn/

Unit 14: Lesson B

Grammar and structures

Should

Husbands **should do** some of the housework.
  (**NOT** ~~Husbands should to do...~~)

Words and expressions to learn

housewife /'haʊswaɪf/
wage /weɪdʒ/
housework /'haʊswɜ:k/
support /sə'pɔ:t/
own /əʊn/
regular /'regjʊlə(r)/
upset /ʌp'set/
special /'speʃl/
free /fri:/
nowadays /'naʊədeɪz/
pocket money /'pɒkɪt 'mʌni/
(fifteen)-year-old
  /(fɪf'ti:n) jɪər 'əʊld/
You're right. /jɔ: 'raɪt/

Revision vocabulary: do you know these words?

midnight /'mɪdnaɪt/
foot (*plural* feet) /fʊt (fi:t)/
school /sku:l/
disco /'dɪskəʊ/
end /end/
pay /peɪ/
stay /steɪ/
agree /ə'gri:/
think (thought, thought) /θɪŋk (θɔ:t)/
choose (chose, chosen) /tʃu:z (tʃəʊz, 'tʃəʊzn)/
enough /ɪ'nʌf/
true /tru:/
early /'ɜ:li/
late /leɪt/
of course /əv 'kɔ:s/
perhaps /pə'hæps/
it depends /ɪt dɪ'pendz/
definitely /'defənətli/

Unit 15: Lesson A

Grammar and structures

Would like

Would you **like** to have a white Rolls Royce?
  No, I **wouldn't**. / Yes, I **would**.
I'd like to be very rich.
Everybody **would like** to speak a lot of languages.

Want

I **wanted to study** Spanish, but my teachers **wanted me to study** Latin.
  (**NOT** ~~my teachers wanted that I study...~~)

Other ways of expressing wishes and hopes

I'm going to try to learn another language before I'm 30.
I hope to finish paying for my car by the end of the year.

By

I'll be there **by** three o'clock. (=at or before three, but not later)

Words and expressions to learn

museum /mju:'zi:əm/
the moon /ðə 'mu:n/
Japan /dʒə'pæn/
magazine /mægə'zi:n/
patience /'peɪʃəns/
artist /'ɑ:tɪst/
midday /mɪd'deɪ/
own (verb) /əʊn/
good at /'gʊd ət/
open (adjective) /'əʊpn/
different (= other) /'dɪfrənt/
political /pə'lɪtɪkl/
really /'rɪəli/
again (=as before) /ə'gen/
everyone /'evrɪwʌn/
by (with time expressions) /baɪ/

145

Unit 15: Lesson B

Grammar and structures

Want + object + infinitive
They **want him to give** them some water.
   (NOT ~~They want that he gives them...~~)

Wondered if + past tense
We **wondered if** we **could** sleep in your barn.
I **wondered if** you **were** free.

Words and expressions to learn

favour /ˈfeɪvə(r)/
Could you do me a favour?
letter /ˈletə(r)/
post (verb) /pəʊst/
Sure (of course) /ʃɔː(r)/
well, ... /wel/
the thing is, ... /ðə ˈθɪŋ ˈɪz/
Thanks a lot.

short of money
That's all right.
you see, ... /juː ˈsiː/
it's like this
We wondered if we could...
Not at all. /nɒt ət ˈɔːl/
this way

Unit 16: Lesson A

Grammar and structures

Quantities
They spend **too much** on tobacco.
They don't spend **enough** on food.
They spent **less** on clothing than on transport.
They spent **more** on food than on housing.
How much is £6 in your currency?
I've spent **a lot of** money on clothes.
   (NOT ~~I've spent much money...~~)
I haven't spent **much** on furniture.
I spent **a lot** on transport last year.
   (NOT ~~I spent much on...~~)
She must travel **less**.

Saying amounts of money
£5.25 = 'five pounds and twenty-five pence' or
'five (pounds) twenty-five'

No article with general meanings
They spent a lot on **food**. (NOT ~~...on the food.~~)
Alcohol and **tobacco** together cost less than half
   as much as housing.
   (NOT ~~The alcohol and the tobacco...~~)

Must and ***can***
Alice **must** spend less on clothing.
   (NOT ~~Alice must to spend...~~)
We **can** spend more on entertainment next year.
   (NOT ~~We can to spend...~~)

Use of verb tenses with time expressions
This year **I've spent** a lot of money on...
Last year **I spent** a lot on...
Next year **I must spend** less on...
Next year **I can spend** more on...

Words and expressions to learn

electricity /ɪlekˈtrɪsəti/
goods /gʊdz/
transport /ˈtrænspɔːt/
opinion /əˈpɪnjən/
currency /ˈkʌrənsi/
budget /ˈbʌdʒɪt/
rent /rent/
savings /ˈseɪvɪŋz/
income /ˈɪnkʌm/
earn /ɜːn/
spend (spent, spent) /spend (spent)/
miscellaneous /mɪsəˈleɪnɪəs/
personal /ˈpɜːsənʊl/
exchange rate /ɪksˈtʃeɪndʒ ˈreɪt/

Learn three or more of these:
fuel /ˈfjuːəl/
tobacco /təˈbækəʊ/
clothing /ˈkləʊðɪŋ/
services /ˈsɜːvɪsɪz/
alcohol /ˈælkəhɒl/
communication /kəmjuːnɪˈkeɪʃn/

Unit 16: Lesson B

Grammar and structures

Making proposals
I'll give you twenty-five pounds.
I'll tell you what.

Quantifiers
If you eat **too much** chocolate, you'll get fat.
I've got **too many** books – I don't know where
   to put them all.
'You can have it for thirty-five.' 'No, that's still
   too much.'

Too... and ***not...enough***
It's **too** heavy to carry.
It's **not** big **enough** to hold all my books.

Words and expressions to learn

pound (weight) /paʊnd/
cover /ˈkʌvə(r)/
drawer /drɔː(r)/
chest of drawers /ˈtʃest əv ˈdrɔːz/
portable /ˈpɔːtəbl/
worth /wɜːθ/
since (=because) /sɪns/
a friend of mine /ə ˈfrend əv ˈmaɪn/
can('t) afford /kn (ˈkɑːnt) əˈfɔːd/
in... condition /ɪn... kənˈdɪʃn/
Come on. /ˈkʌm ˈɒn/
I'll tell you what. /aɪl ˈtel juː ˈwɒt/
To tell you the truth, ... /tə ˈtel juː ðə ˈtruːθ/
Oh, very well. /ˈəʊ ˈveri ˈwel/
I'd prefer... /aɪd prɪˈfɜː(r)/
if you don't mind /ɪf juː ˈdəʊnt ˈmaɪnd/

Revision vocabulary: do you know these words?

old /əʊld/
fat /fæt/
heavy /ˈhevi/
strong /strɒŋ/
difficult /ˈdɪfɪkʊlt/
long /lɒŋ/
small /smɔːl/

Unit 17: Lesson A

Grammar and structures

Time clauses
I usually read for a bit **before I go to sleep**.
Before I go to sleep, I usually read for a bit.
I enjoyed life more **after I left school**.
After I left school, I enjoyed life more.
Give John my love **when you see him**.
When you see John, give him my love.
I'll phone you **as soon as I arrive**.
    (NOT ~~as soon as I will arrive.~~)
As soon as I arrive, I'll phone you.
I'll wait **until you're ready**.

Still, yet and *already*
John's **still** in bed.
He hasn't got up **yet**.
Susan is **already** dressed.

So and *such*
so handsome
such a handsome man
so quiet
such a quiet life
so kind to her
such a kind person
so good
such good bread
so happy
such happy people

Words and expressions to learn
postman /ˈpəʊstmən/
mat /mæt/
commercial traveller /kəˈmɜːʃl ˈtrævlə(r)/
make a bed /ˈmeɪk ə ˈbed/
undress /ʌnˈdres/
brush one's teeth /ˈbrʌʃ wʌnz ˈtiːθ/
put out (a light) (put, put) /ˈpʊt ˈaʊt/
go to bed (went, gone) /ˈgəʊ tə ˈbed (went, gɒn)/
address (a letter) /əˈdres/
answer (a letter) /ˈɑːnsə(r)/
translate /trænzˈleɪt/
keep on (kept, kept) (...ing) /ˈkiːp ˈɒn (kept)/
report /rɪˈpɔːt/
as many as possible /əz ˈmeni əz ˈpɒsəbl/

Unit 17: Lesson B

Grammar and structures

Past perfect tense

I had (I'd) gone
you had (you'd) gone
he/she/it had (he'd/she'd/it'd) gone
we had (we'd) gone
they had (they'd) gone

had I gone?
had you gone?
had he/she/it gone?
had we gone?
had they gone?

I had not (hadn't) gone
you had not (hadn't) gone
he/she/it had not (hadn't) gone
we had not (hadn't) gone
they had not (hadn't) gone

Simple past and past perfect

PAST (THEN):	I **saw** who it was
EARLIER PAST (BEFORE THEN):	I **hadn't seen** her for a very long time
PAST:	We **talked** about...
EARLIER PAST:	...the hopes we**'d shared**.

Words and expressions to learn
the way (to somewhere) /ðə ˈweɪ/
directions /dəˈrekʃnz/
recognition /rekəgˈnɪʃn/
silence /ˈsaɪləns/
ghost /gəʊst/
feelings /ˈfiːlɪŋz/
the good old days /ðə ˈgʊd ˈəʊld ˈdeɪz/
hope /həʊp/
meeting /ˈmiːtɪŋ/
look /lʊk/
realise /ˈrɪəlaɪz/
lead (led, led) /liːd (led)/
go wrong (went, gone) /ˈgəʊ ˈrɒŋ (went, gɒn)/
reserve /rɪˈzɜːv/
examine /ɪgˈzæmɪn/
repair /rɪˈpeə(r)/
pleased /pliːzd/

Unit 18: Lesson A

Grammar and structures

Direct speech and reported speech
They thought 'The sun **goes** round the earth'.
They ***thought*** that the sun ***went*** round the earth.

    (NOT ~~They thought that the sun goes~~)
Galileo said, 'Light and heavy things **fall** at the same speed'.
Galileo ***said*** that light and heavy things ***fell*** at the same speed.

Reported questions
They wondered **if/whether** Aristotle was right.
Do you know **whether** Britain has a king **or** a queen?
She asked **what my name was**.
    (NOT ~~what was my name.~~)
Do you know **where she lives**?
    (NOT ~~where does she live?~~)

Words and expressions to learn
the blood /ðə ˈblʌd/
illness /ˈɪlnɪs/
star /stɑː(r)/
scientist /ˈsaɪəntɪst/
religion /rɪˈlɪdʒən/
politics /ˈpɒlətɪks/
animal /ˈænɪml/
war /wɔː(r)/
experiment /ɪksˈperɪmənt/
cause /kɔːz/
tell a lie (told, told) /ˈtel ə ˈlaɪ (təʊld)/
discover /dɪsˈkʌvə(r)/
flat /flæt/
living /ˈlɪvɪŋ/
equal /ˈiːkwəl/
impossible /ɪmˈpɒsəbl/

Unit 18: Lesson B

Grammar and structures

Modal verbs: probability and certainty
It **must** be late – it's getting dark.
It **might** be true, but I don't think it is.
She **can't** be English – she's got a French accent.
'Who's at the door?' 'It **could** be the postman.'

Likely
I'm likely to be in London next Tuesday. Can I get you
 anything?
Do you think it**'s likely to rain**?
There is likely to be a meeting on Tuesday.
There are likely to be about 20 people at the meeting.

Say and *tell*
Fred **said** that he was a photographer.
Fred **told Janet** that he was a photographer.
 (**NOT** Fred told that...)
 (**NOT** Fred said Janet that...)

Words and expressions to learn

full name /ˈfʊl ˈneɪm/
profession /prəˈfeʃn/
poetry /ˈpəʊətri/
parking place /ˈpɑːkɪŋ ˈpleɪs/
photograph /ˈfəʊtəgrɑːf/
likely /ˈlaɪkli/
none /nʌn/

Learn some words from the text about the Amazon Forest.

Revision vocabulary: do you know these words?

age /eɪdʒ/
address /əˈdres/
interest /ˈɪntrəst/
education /edjʊˈkeɪʃn/
qualifications /kwɒlɪfɪˈkeɪʃnz/
spring /sprɪŋ/
phone call /ˈfəʊn ˈkɔːl/
election /ɪˈlekʃn/
say (said, said) /seɪ (sed)/

tell (told, told) /tel (təʊld)/
travel /ˈtrævl/
happen /ˈhæpn/
true /truː/
famous /ˈfeɪməs/
strange /streɪndʒ/
wet /wet/
by (=not later than) /baɪ/

Unit 19: Lesson A

Grammar and structures

Question-tags
You're German, **aren't you?**
You've changed the room round, **haven't you?**
She can speak Arabic, **can't she?**
Your wife smokes, doesn't she?
The film started late, **didn't it?**

Place of prepositions in questions
What are you talking **about?**
 (**NOT** About what are you talking?)
What are you looking **at?**
Who did she go **with?**
Who are you looking **for?**

Words and expressions to learn

sofa /ˈsəʊfə/
coat /kəʊt/
ground /graʊnd/
weekday /ˈwiːkdeɪ/
a change /ə ˈtʃeɪndʒ/
move /muːv/
ask for /ˈɑːsk fə(r)/
delicious /dɪˈlɪʃəs/
hard work
somewhere else
I beg your pardon? /aɪ ˈbeg jə ˈpɑːdn/
I should think
How do you mean?

Could you pass me...
I've had enough
How stupid of me!

Learn two or more of these:
mustard /ˈmʌstəd/
meat /miːt/
bean /biːn/
carrot /ˈkærət/
wine /waɪn/

Unit 19: Lesson B

Grammar and structures

Agreeing and disagreeing with opinions
I like...
I quite like...
I really like...
I like... very much.
I love...

So do I.
I don't.
I quite like him/her/
 it/them.
I've never heard of him/
 her/it/them.

So do I, Neither do I, etc.
'**I like** traditional jazz.' '**So do I.**'
'**I don't like** science fiction.' '**Neither do I.**'
'**Sarah is** tired.' '**So is Sally.**'
'**We're not** hungry.' '**Neither are we.**'
'**I've got** a headache.' '**So have I.**'
'**They haven't got** a car.' '**Neither have we.**'
'**Tim saw** Ann yesterday.' '**So did I.**'
'**I didn't have** a holiday last year.' '**Neither did I.**'
'**My brother will be** 35 next month.' '**So will I!**'
'**I won't be** here for the meeting.' '**Neither will I.**'
'**Tom was** fairer when he was a child.' '**So was Ruth.**'
'**You weren't** here when he came.' '**Neither were you.**'

Words and expressions to learn

sex /seks/
violence /ˈvaɪələns/
complete /kəmˈpliːt/
awful /ˈɔːfʊl/
old-fashioned /ˈəʊld ˈfæʃənd/
whose /huːz/
I didn't think much of it.
I couldn't help it.
It's getting late.
We've got a long way to go.
We ought to be on our way.
I suppose
We'd better be going.
enjoy myself/yourself/etc.
Thank you for coming.
I'll give you a ring.
Thank you so much.

Revision vocabulary: do you know these words?

beginning /bɪˈgɪnɪŋ/
middle /ˈmɪdl/
end /end/
food /fuːd/
coffee /ˈkɒfi/
die /daɪ/
laugh /lɑːf/
spend (spent, spent)
 /spend (spent)/
dirty /ˈdɜːti/
mine /maɪn/
I can't stand...
See you next week.

Unit 20: Lesson A

Grammar and structures

Infinitive of purpose
To make tomatoes easier to peel, cover them...
(NOT ~~For to make...~~)

By...ing
You can clean dirty saucepans **by filling** them with cold water and vinegar and letting them boil for five minutes.

Had better
I **had** (**I'd**) **better** phone my sister.
(NOT ~~I'd better to phone...~~)
(NOT ~~I have better...~~)
You **had** (**You'd**) **better** phone your sister. etc.

Had I **better** phone her now?
Had you **better** phone her now? etc.

I **had** (**I'd**) **better not** wait any longer.
(NOT ~~I hadn't better...~~)
You **had** (**you'd**) **better not** wait any longer. etc.

Words and expressions to learn

finger /'fɪŋgə(r)/
rabbit /'ræbɪt/
saucepan /'sɔ:spən/
dust /dʌst/
rice /raɪs/
scratch /skrætʃ/
luggage /'lʌgɪdʒ/
examination /ɪgzæmɪ'neɪʃn/
peel /pi:l/
rub /rʌb/
shake (shook, shaken) /ʃeɪk (ʃʊk, 'ʃeɪkn)/
stick (stuck, stuck) /stɪk (stʌk)/
catch (caught, caught) /kætʃ (kɔ:t)/
empty /'empti/
tight /taɪt/
pregnant /'pregnənt/

Revision vocabulary: do you know these words?

tomato /tə'mɑ:təʊ/
guitar /gɪ'tɑ:(r)/
glass /glɑ:s/
newspaper /'nju:speɪpə(r)/
ear /ɪə(r)/
potato /pə'teɪtəʊ/
apple /'æpl/
beer /bɪə(r)/
yard /jɑ:d/
ring (rang, rung) /rɪŋ (ræŋ, rʌŋ)/
cover /'kʌvə(r)/
wash /wɒʃ/
pick up /'pɪk 'ʌp/
visit /'vɪzɪt/
dirty /'dɜ:ti/
together /tə'geðə(r)/
comfortable /'kʌmftəbl/
wet /wet/

Unit 20: Lesson B

Grammar and structures

Suggestions
If I were you, I'd turn it the other way round.
I think you ought to turn it upside down.
Why don't you turn it sideways?
Let's help him.

If + 'unreal' conditions
If I **were** you, I'd (I **would**) turn it the other way round.
It **would be** much better if he **turned** it back to front.
What **would** you **do** if you **had** this mess in your kitchen?
I **wouldn't do** it like that if I **were** you.
Wouldn't you?

Ought to
You **ought to** turn it upside down.
She **ought to** be able to get one free.
(NOT ~~She oughts to...~~)

Imperatives + or
Put a blanket underneath it **or** it'll get dirty.
Cover it **or** it'll get wet.

Remember to, forget to
Remember to cover it...
Don't **forget to** tighten all the screws.

Words and expressions to learn

screw /skru:/
law /lɔ:/
drug /drʌg/
give up (gave, given) /'gɪv 'ʌp (geɪv, 'gɪvn)/
seem /si:m/
immediately /ɪ'mi:dɪətli/
back to front /'bæk tə 'frʌnt/
face downwards /'feɪs 'daʊnwədz/
inside out /'ɪnsaɪd 'aʊt/
sideways /'saɪdweɪz/
underneath /ʌndə'ni:θ/
upside down /'ʌpsaɪd 'daʊn/
the other way round /ði 'ʌðə 'weɪ 'raʊnd/
this way /'ðɪs 'weɪ/
I'll think about it. /aɪl 'θɪŋk ə'baʊt ɪt/
It's no trouble. /ɪts 'nəʊ 'trʌbl/

Unit 21: Lesson A

Grammar and structures

Must and mustn't
In Britain you **must** buy a licence if you have a TV.
(NOT ~~you must to buy...~~)
You **must** unplug an electrical appliance before you try to repair it.
You **mustn't** touch anything electrical if you are in the bath.

Phrasal verbs
Switch on the radio. **Switch** the radio **on**.
Switch it **on**. (NOT ~~Switch on it.~~)
Turn up the TV. **Turn** the TV **up**.
Turn it **up**. (NOT ~~Turn up it.~~)

Which (of)
Which would you choose?
Which colour would you like?

Which of the things in the picture would you like?
Which of them would you like?

Words and expressions to learn

plug in /'plʌg 'ɪn/
unplug /ʌn'plʌg/
turn up /'tɜ:n 'ʌp/
turn down /'tɜ:n 'daʊn/

Learn some of these:
tape recorder /'teɪp rɪ'kɔ:də(r)/
stereo /'sterɪəʊ/
record player /'rekɔ:d 'pleɪə(r)/
cassette player /kə'set 'pleɪə(r)/
vacuum cleaner /'vækjuəm 'kli:nə(r)/
hair dryer /'heə 'draɪə(r)/
washing machine /'wɒʃɪŋ mə'ʃi:n/

dishwasher /'dɪʃwɒʃə(r)/
mixer /'mɪksə(r)/
dryer /'draɪə(r)/
heater /'hi:tə(r)/
cooker /'kʊkə(r)/
iron /'aɪən/
toaster /'təʊstə(r)/
bulb /bʌlb/

knob /nɒb/
plug /plʌg/
socket /'sɒkɪt/
lead /li:d/
lamp /læmp/
torch /tɔ:tʃ/
battery /'bætri/
wire /'waɪə(r)/

Unit 21: Lesson B

Grammar and structures

Verb + -ing form
It's **started making** a funny noise.
It **keeps sticking**.
It won't **stop dripping**.

Won't
It **won't** start.

Words and expressions to learn

flash /flæʃ/
engine /'endʒən/
dial /daɪl/
record /rɪ'kɔ:d/
wind (wound, wound) /waɪnd (waʊnd)/
rewind (rewound, rewound)
  /ri:'waɪnd (ri:'waʊnd)/

flood /flʌd/
keep (kept, kept) /ki:p (kept)/
ring (rang, rung) /rɪŋ (ræŋ, rʌŋ)/
leak /li:k/
properly /'prɒpəli/
take a photo
there's something wrong with...

Unit 22: Lesson A

Spelling and pronunciation

Two syllables, not three: asp(i)rin, bus(i)ness, cam(e)ra, diff(e)rent, ev(e)ning, ev(e)ry, marri(a)ge, med(i)cine.

Three syllables, not four: comf(or)table, secret(a)ry, temp(e)rature, veg(e)table, usu(a)lly.

Silent letters: shou(l)d, cou(l)d, wou(l)d, ca(l)m, wa(l)k, ta(l)k, ha(l)f, i(r)on, i(s)land, lis(t)en, (w)rite, (w)rong, (k)now, (k)nife, (k)nee, (k)nock, (k)nob, dau(gh)ter, hei(gh)t, li(gh)t, mi(gh)t, ri(gh)t, ti(gh)t, strai(gh)t, throu(gh), wei(gh), nei(gh)bour, ou(gh)t, thou(gh)t, g(u)ess, g(u)ide, g(u)itar, (h)our, (h)onest, We(d)n(e)sday, san(d)wich, si(g)n.

gh = /f/   cough, enough, laugh.
ch = /k/   chemist, headache, toothache, stomach, school, scheme.
a = /e/   any, many
ea = /e/   bread, breakfast, dead, death, head, health, heavy, instead, leather, pleasure, ready, sweater.
ea = /eɪ/   steak, break.
o = /ʌ/   brother, come, company, cover, government, love, money, month, mother, nothing, one, onion, other, some, son, stomach, wonder, worry.
ou = /ʌ/   country, couple, cousin, double, enough, trouble.
u = /ʊ/   butcher, pull, push, put.

All these words are pronounced with /aɪ/: dial, either, neither, buy, height, idea, iron, microphone.

Strange spellings:

area /'eərɪə/
Asia /'eɪʃə/
Australia /ɒs'treɪlɪə/
autumn /'ɔ:təm/
bicycle /'baɪsɪkl/
blood /blʌd/
biscuit /'bɪskɪt/
busy /'bɪzi/

Europe /'jʊərəp/
foreign /'fɒrən/
friend /frend/
fruit /fru:t/
heard /hɜ:d/
heart /hɑ:t/
juice /dʒu:s/
minute /'mɪnɪt/

moustache /mə'stɑ:ʃ/
one /wʌn/
people /'pi:pl/
sandwich /'sænwɪdʒ/
theatre /'θɪətə(r)/
two /tu:/
woman /'wʊmən/
women /'wɪmɪn/

> THERE IS NO SUMMARY FOR
> UNIT 22, LESSON B

Unit 23: Lesson A

Grammar and structures

Let + object + infinitive
I never **let my emotions build up** inside me.
  (NOT ~~... let my emotions to build up...~~)
  (NOT ~~... let that my emotions build up...~~)

Words and expressions to learn

mood /mu:d/
secret /'si:krɪt/
smile /smaɪl/
frown /fraʊn/
build up (built, built) /bɪld 'ʌp (bɪlt)/
get over /'get 'əʊvə(r)/
shout /ʃaʊt/
let (let, let) /let/
hide (hid, hidden) /haɪd (hɪd, 'hɪdn)/

afraid /ə'freɪd/
relaxed /rɪ'lækst/
amused /ə'mju:zd/
sad /sæd/
easy-going /'i:zi 'gəʊɪŋ/
good/bad times /'gʊd/'bæd 'taɪmz/

> **Learn two or more of these:**
> emotion /ɪ'məʊʃn/
> express /ɪk'spres/
> emotional /ɪ'məʊʃənl/
> Damn you! /'dæm ju:/
> Oh dear! /'əʊ 'dɪə(r)/
> You're kidding. /jɔ: 'kɪdɪŋ/

Revision vocabulary:
do you know these words?

problem /'prɒbləm/
laugh /lɑ:f/
cry /kraɪ/
upset (upset, upset) /ʌp'set/
share /ʃeə(r)/
feel (felt, felt) /fi:l (felt)/
angry /'æŋgri/
worried /'wʌrɪd/
pleased /pli:zd/
surprised /sə'praɪzd/
calm /kɑ:m/

Unit 23: Lesson B

Grammar and structures

Who as subject and object

Who **loves** John?
Who **does** John love?
Who **saw** you?
Who **did** you see?
Who**'s waiting for** you?
Who **are** you **waiting for**?

Words and expressions to learn

programme /'prəʊgræm/
relationship /rɪ'leɪʃənʃɪp/
dislike /dɪs'laɪk/
admire /əd'maɪə(r)/
grow (grew, grown) (=become) /grəʊ (gru:, grəʊn)/
last /lɑ:st/
get to know /'get tə 'nəʊ/
fond of /'fɒnd əv/

close /kləʊs/
lucky /'lʌki/
silly /'sɪli/
guilty /'gɪlti/
whole /həʊl/
strongly /'strɒŋli/
in love /ɪn 'lʌv/

Unit 24: Lesson A

Grammar and structures

Countable and uncountable nouns

Countable nouns have plurals, and can be used with *a/an*. Examples: road house member cabinet idea.

Uncountable nouns have no plurals, and cannot be used with *a/an*. Examples: education power water music meat.

Note that these are uncountable in English:
English information luggage news travel hair weather.

Who and *which*

***Who* is used for people, and *which* for things.**

The President of Fantasia, **who** is paid a very high salary, is elected for life.
San Fantastico, **which** is the capital of Fantasia, is the centre of government.

Words and expressions to learn

authority /ɔ:'θɒrəti/
government /'gʌvəmənt/
capital /'kæpɪtl/
Parliament /'pɑ:lɪmənt/
power /'paʊə(r)/
MP /'em'pi:/
area /'eərɪə/
leader /'li:də(r)/
majority /mə'dʒɒrəti/
party /'pɑ:ti/
Prime Minister /'praɪm 'mɪnɪstə(r)/
department /dɪ'pɑ:tmənt/
news /nju:z/
elect /ɪ'lekt/
local /'ləʊkl/
responsible (for) /rɪ'spɒnsəbl/
main /meɪn/

Unit 24: Lesson B

Grammar and structures

Imperatives
Affirmative imperative: Be careful.
Negative imperative: Don't be silly.
Emphatic imperative: Do be careful.

Reported commands and requests
His mother **told him to tidy up** afterwards.
She **told him not to invite** the Edwards boy.
(**NOT** to not invite...)

Question-tags after negative sentences
You**'re not** going to invite that Edwards boy, **are you**?
You **won't** play your father's jazz records, **will you**?

Question-tags after imperatives
See that that letter goes today, **will you**?
(**More polite: See...**, **would you**?)
Don't make too much noise, **will you**?

Words and expressions to learn

carpet /'kɑ:pɪt/
jazz /dʒæz/
noise /nɔɪz/
order /'ɔ:də(r)/
delivery /dɪ'lɪvri/
part /pɑ:t/
invite /ɪn'vaɪt/
promise /'prɒmɪs/

tidy up /'taɪdi 'ʌp/
urgent /'ɜ:dʒənt/
last time /'lɑ:st 'taɪm/
I suppose so /aɪ sə'pəʊz səʊ/
see that... /'si: ðət/
exactly /ɪg'zæktli/
out of the question

Unit 25: Lesson A

Grammar and structures

Word order: Object just after verb
I **like the Hilliard picture** very much.
(**NOT** I like very much the Hilliard picture.)
I **like the snow picture** best.
I **don't like the picture** of the young man much.
(**NOT** I don't like much...)

Very and too
I think Sylvia von Harden's face is **very** interesting.
I don't like the colours in the picture of the woman; they're **too** strong.

People who do things (*-er*)
A person who **drives** is a **driver**.
A person who **paints** is a **painter**.

Questions ending in *by*
Who was *The Third Man* directed **by**?
(**NOT** By who was...) (**NOT** By whom was...)

→

Words and expressions to learn

snow /snəʊ/
leaf (leaves) /li:f (li:vz)/
painting /'peɪntɪŋ/
writer /'raɪtə(r)/

director /dɪ'rektə(r)/
actor /'æktə(r)/
art /ɑ:t/
statue /'stætʃu:/

play /pleɪ/
return (verb) /rɪ'tɜ:n/
modern /'mɒdn/
real /rɪəl/

public /'pʌblɪk/
great /greɪt/
so-called /'səʊ 'kɔ:ld/
work of art /'wɜ:k əv 'ɑ:t/

Unit 25: Lesson B

Grammar and structures

Asking for suggestions
Where **shall** we go, then?

Making suggestions
How about a concert?
What about Stravinsky, then?
Why don't we have a drink somewhere first?

Which and *What*
Which of the three songs do you prefer?
What sort of music do you like?

The one/the ones
'Which record shall I put on?' '**The** new **one**.'
'Which seats are ours?' '**The ones** near the front.'

Words and expressions to learn

tune /tju:n/
voice /vɔɪs/
verse /vɜ:s/
concert /'kɒnsət/
stairs /steəz/
folk (music) /fəʊk/
mad (about) /mæd/
sentimental /sentɪ'mentl/
lonely /'ləʊnli/
then /ðen/
what's on /'wɒts 'ɒn/
Here we are. (=Here it is.)
  /'hɪə wi 'ɑ:(r)/
quite a /'kwaɪt ə/

otherwise /'ʌðəwaɪz/
What about...? /'wɒt ə'baʊt/
plenty of /'plenti əv/

Revision vocabulary: do you know these words?

choice /tʃɔɪs/
instrument /'ɪnstrəmənt/
music /'mju:zɪk/
piano /pi'ænəʊ/
violin /vaɪə'lɪn/
trumpet /'trʌmpɪt/
guitar /gɪ'tɑ:(r)/

Unit 26: Lesson A

Grammar and structures

Although /ɔ:l'ðəʊ/
Whales are mammals, **although** they look like fish.
Although whales look like fish, they are mammals.
  (**NOT** ~~Although whales look like fish, but they...~~)

He lost his job **although** he worked well.
Although he worked well, he lost his job.

Words and expressions to learn

insect /'ɪnsekt/
skeleton /'skelɪtn/
backbone /'bækbəʊn/
belong (to) /bɪ'lɒŋ (tə)/
typical /'tɪpɪkl/
related (to) /rɪ'leɪtɪd (tə)/
divided (into) /dɪ'vaɪdɪd ('ɪntə)/
except for /ɪk'sept fə(r)/
in many ways

Revision vocabulary: do you know these words?

dog /dɒg/
animal /'ænɪml/
fish /fɪʃ/
bird /bɜ:d/
kind /kaɪnd/
difference /'dɪfrəns/
group /gru:p/
different /'dɪfrənt/
main /meɪn/

Unit 26: Lesson B

Words and expressions to learn

bookcase /'bʊkeɪs/
wardrobe /'wɔ:drəʊb/
mouse /maʊs/
camel /'kæml/
lion /'laɪən/

cow /kaʊ/
India /'ɪndɪə/
China /'tʃaɪnə/
France /frɑ:ns/
Egypt /'i:dʒɪpt/

Israel /'ɪzreɪl/
strawberry /'strɔ:bri/
grape /greɪp/
peach /pi:tʃ/
armchair /'ɑ:mtʃeə(r)/

Revision vocabulary: do you know these words?

nose /nəʊz/
ear /ɪə(r)/
arm /ɑ:m/
hand /hænd/
mouth /maʊθ/
foot /fʊt/
mistake /mɪs'teɪk/

Unit 27: Lesson A

Grammar and structures

Get to talk about changes
He'*s got* more popular.
It'*ll get* dirty.

Words and expressions to learn

wrinkle /'rɪŋkl/
beard /bɪəd/
moustache /məs'tɑ:ʃ/
childhood /'tʃaɪldhʊd/
adolescence /ædə'lesəns/
break (broke, broken)
  /breɪk (brəʊk, 'brəʊkn)/
rust /rʌst/
crack /kræk/

wear (down) (wore, worn) /weə(r) (wɔ:(r), wɔ:n)/
gain weight /'geɪn 'weɪt/
lose weight (lost, lost) /'lu:z 'weɪt (lɒst)/
bald /bɔ:ld/
go grey/bald (went, gone)
  /gəʊ 'greɪ/bɔ:ld (went, gɒn)/
middle age /'mɪdl 'eɪdʒ/
old age /'əʊld 'eɪdʒ/

Unit 27: Lesson B

Grammar and structures

Past conditional
If he **'d studied** literature, he **would have become** a journalist.
If his parents **had been** well off, he **wouldn't have worked** in a bank.
The woman's arm **wouldn't have been burnt** if the car **hadn't crashed.**

Words and expressions to learn

literature /'lɪtrətʃə(r)/
physics /'fɪzɪks/
research /rɪ'sɜ:tʃ/
prisoner /'prɪznə(r)/
sausage /'sɒsɪdʒ/
stand /stænd/
chip /tʃɪp/
pavement /'peɪvmənt/

escape /ɪ'skeɪp/
bite (bit, bitten) /baɪt (bɪt, 'bɪtn)/
faint /feɪnt/
feel sorry for (felt, felt) /'fi:l 'sɒri fə(r) (felt)/
well off /'wel 'ɒf/
working class /'wɜ:kɪŋ 'klɑ:s/
wild /waɪld/

Revision vocabulary: do you know these words?

decide /dɪ'saɪd/
scratch /skrætʃ/
cause /kɔ:z/
crash /kræʃ/
boil /bɔɪl/
burn (burnt, burnt) /bɜ:n (bɜ:nt)/
wait (for) /'weɪt (fə(r))/
hurt (hurt, hurt) /hɜ:t/
fall (fell, fallen) /fɔ:l (fel, 'fɔ:lən)/
angry /'æŋgri/
local /'ləʊkl/
university /ju:nɪ'vɜ:sɪti/
war /wɔ:(r)/
bring (brought, brought) /brɪŋ (brɔ:t)/
find (found, found) /faɪnd (faʊnd)/
fall in love

Unit 28: Lesson A

Grammar and structures

-ing forms
Eating good quality food is the most important thing you can do...
  (NOT To eat good quality food...)
The things I do to take care of my health are: **not smoking,** ...

Relative clauses
A friend **who had similar problems** made her think she might have allergies.
  (NOT A friend who she had similar problems...)
She has to avoid the things **that make her ill.**
  (NOT ... the things that they make her ill.)
The pills **her doctor gave her** only worked for a short while.

Verbs with two objects
I would give **him a book** on exercise.
I would tell **her horrible stories...**

Some verbs that can be used with two objects are:
bring, buy, give, lend, make, owe, promise, read, send, show, take, tell, write.

Words and expressions to learn

exercise /'eksəsaɪz/
quality /'kwɒləti/
headache /'hedeɪk/
while /waɪl/
(a good) example /ɪg'zɑ:mpl/
present /'prezənt/
diet /'daɪət/
keep (kept, kept) /ki:p (kept)/
concentrate /'kɒnsəntreɪt/
avoid /ə'vɔɪd/
pollute /pə'lu:t/
complicate /'kɒmplɪkeɪt/
promise /'prɒmɪs/
heart attack /'hɑ:t ə'tæk/
horrible /'hɒrəbl/

Revision vocabulary: do you know these words?

health /helθ/
weight /weɪt/
alcohol /'ælkəhɒl/
medicine /'medsən/
chemicals /'kemɪklz/
advertisement /əd'vɜ:tɪsmənt/
smoke /sməʊk/

Unit 28: Lesson B

Grammar and structures

Where to put frequency adverbs in a sentence
These adverbs say how often something happens: *usually, sometimes, often, always, ever, never.* They can go in mid-position in a sentence (after auxiliary verbs and *am, are, is, was* and *were*; before other verbs).

Do you **sometimes** feel sleepy after eating?
  (NOT Do you feel sometimes sleepy...)
  (NOT Do you feel sleepy after eating sometimes?)
She's **always** in a great hurry.
I **often** eat very quickly.

Often, sometimes and *usually* can go at the beginning of a clause, to make their meaning more important.

Sometimes I get upset if I have to wait in a queue.
  (NOT Always I get upset if I...)

153

Where to put adverbial phrases and clauses in a sentence

Adverbial phrases and clauses (like these from the lesson: *every year, three or four times a week, when you walk, the whole time, all the time*) can go at the end of the sentence; or at the beginning of the sentence followed by a comma.

It happens **every year**.
  (**NOT** It every year happens.)
The whole time, I feel sort of funny.
  (**NOT** The whole time I feel sort of funny.)

Reporting orders and advice

'Now just lie down here.' He **told me to lie** down.

'Don't carry heavy things for a while.'
He **told me not to carry** heavy things for a while.

'I think you should make an appointment at the Eye Hospital.'
He **advised me to make** an appointment at the Eye Hospital.

'You'd better not do any running for a week or so.'
He **advised me not to do** any running for a week or so.

Words and expressions to learn

patient /'peɪʃənt/
chest /tʃest/
pain /peɪn/
muscle /'mʌsl/
operation /ɒpə'reɪʃn/
injection /ɪn'dʒekʃən/
tablet /'tæblɪt/
stand up (stood, stood) /'stænd 'ʌp (stʊd)/
lie down (lay, lain) /'laɪ 'daʊn (leɪ, leɪn)/
itch /ɪtʃ/
bend over (bent, bent) /'bend 'əʊvə(r) (bent)/
advise /əd'vaɪz/

painful /'peɪnfʊl/
How often...? /'haʊ 'ɒfn/
back trouble /'bæk 'trʌbl/
hay fever /'heɪ 'fiːvə(r)/
sore throat /'sɔː 'θrəʊt/

Revision vocabulary: do you know these words?

funny (=strange) /'fʌni/
heavy /'hevi/
downstairs /daʊn'steəz/
inside /ɪn'saɪd/
outside /aʊt'saɪd/
hardly /'haːdli/
exactly /ɪg'zæktli/
sometimes /'sʌmtaɪmz/
often /'ɒfn/
...times a week, day, etc.

Unit 29: Lesson A

Grammar and structures

I wish

I wish I **had** more artistic ability.
I wish I **could** remember people's names.
I wish I **was** (*or* were) better at making decisions.

> THERE IS NO SUMMARY FOR UNIT 29, LESSON B

Words and expressions to learn

brain /breɪn/
imagination /ɪmædʒə'neɪʃn/
ability /ə'bɪləti/
fact /fækt/
common sense /'kɒmən 'sens/
sense of humour /'sens əv 'hjuːmə(r)/
zoo /zuː/
make decisions /'meɪk dɪ'sɪʒənz/
plan /plæn/
deal with (dealt, dealt) /'diːl 'wɪð (delt)/
test /test/
practical /'præktɪkl/

Learn three or more of these:

decisiveness /dɪ'saɪsɪvnəs/
logic /'lɒdʒɪk/
argument /'aːgjəmənt/
quick thinking /'kwɪk 'θɪŋkɪŋ/
analyse /'ænəlaɪz/
calculate /'kælkjəleɪt/
classify /'klæsɪfaɪ/
draw conclusions (drew, drawn) /'drɔː kən'kluːʒənz (druː, drɔːn)/
reorganise /riː'ɔːgenaɪz)/
mathematical /mæθ'mætɪkl/
artistic /aː'tɪstɪk/
smelly /'smeli/

Unit 30: Lesson A

Grammar and structures

Adverbs with past participles

Government ministers are **well paid**.
Farm workers are **badly paid**.
Housewives are **the worst-paid** workers in the world.

Should with passive infinitive

Nurses **should be paid** more.
Primary school teachers **should be paid** more than bus drivers.

-ing forms

Keith **hates not having** enough time to do his job well.
Jane **likes having** to think.
Working with nice people is very important to me.
Getting on with my boss is one of the most important things in a job for me.

Words and expressions to learn

factory /'fæktri/
dustman /'dʌstmən/
army /'aːmi/
pay /peɪ/
professor /prə'fɒsə(r)/
journalist /'dʒɜːnəlɪst/
farm /faːm/
routine /ruː'tiːn/
contact /'kɒntækt/
security /sɪ'kjʊərəti/
pension /'penʃən/
promotion /prə'məʊʃn/
responsibility /rɪspɒnsə'bɪləti/
freedom /'friːdəm/
primary school /'praɪmri 'skuːl/
have (something) in common /'hæv ('sʌmθɪŋ) ɪn 'kɒmən/
retire /rɪ'taɪə(r)/

Unit 30: Lesson B

Grammar and structures

Have to
Do you **have to get up** early?
You mean you **have to go and check**
   that they're actually building the thing?

Words and expressions to learn

team /ti:m/
heater /'hi:tə(r)/
handle /'hændl/
design /dɪ'zaɪn/
waste /weɪst/
check /tʃek/
frustrate /frʌs'treɪt/
work long hours
mad /mæd/
especially /ɪ'speʃli/
on (your) own /'ɒn (jɔ:r) 'əʊn/

Names of professions
Choose five or more of these:
accountant /ə'kaʊntənt/
architect /'ɑ:kɪtekt/
businesswoman /'bɪznɪswʊmən/
coal miner /'kəʊl 'maɪnə(r)/
draughtsman /-woman /'drɑ:ftsmən
   ('drɑ:ftswʊmən)/
electrician /ɪlek'trɪʃn/
(mechanical) engineer /
   (mɪ'kænɪkl) endʒɪ'nɪə(r)/
personnel manager /pɜ:sə'nel 'mænɪdʒə(r)/
photographer /fə'tɒɡrəfə(r)/
sales manager /'seɪlz 'mænɪdʒə(r)/
technician /tek'nɪʃn/

Unit 31: Lesson A

Grammar and structures

Come/go; here/there; this/that
Come over **here** and look at **this.**
Go over **there** and look at **that.**

Words and expressions to learn

tube /tju:b/
take-off /'teɪk 'ɒf/
garage /'gærɑ:ʒ/
petrol station /'petrʊl 'steɪʃn/
enquiry /ɪn'kwaɪəri/

compartment /kəm'pɑ:tmənt/
roundabout /'raʊndəbaʊt/
speed /spi:d/
land /lænd/
delay /dɪ'leɪ/

Unit 31: Lesson B

Grammar and structures

Modals of obligation

Must, can and *should* are 'modal' verbs. They have no
-s in the third person singular; questions and
negatives are formed without *do*; and they are followed
by the infinitive without *to.*

She **should** report the accident.
   (NOT She shoulds...)
You **must not** drive without lights at night.
   (NOT You don't must drive...)
Can you **park** on a single yellow line?
   (NOT Do you can...)
You **cannot turn** right here.
   (NOT You cannot to turn...)

Words and expressions to learn

(road) sign /saɪn/
traffic /'træfɪk/
pedestrian /pə'destrɪən/
pedestrian crossing /pə'destrɪən 'krɒsɪŋ/
junction /'dʒʌŋkʃən/
the right of way /ðə 'raɪt əv 'weɪ/
diagram /'daɪəɡræm/
regulation /regjə'leɪʃn/

overtake (overtook, overtaken)
   /əʊvə'teɪk (əʊvə'tʊk, əʊvo'teɪkn)/
park (verb) /pɑ:k/
approach /ə'prəʊtʃ/
clear /'klɪə(r)/
slippery /'slɪpəri/
in the opposite direction

Unit 32: Lesson A

Grammar and structures

Sound + adjective
She **sounds** surprised.
You **sound** happy.

Make + object + infinitive
It **makes** me laugh.

Find + object + adjective
I don't **find** it funny.
Do you **find** this cartoon silly?

THERE IS NO SUMMARY FOR
UNIT 32, LESSON B

Words and expressions to learn

doorbell /'dɔ:bel/
(newspaper) headline /'hedlaɪn/
reaction /ri'ækʃn/
result /rɪ'zʌlt/
specialise (in) /'speʃəlaɪz/
bet (bet, bet) /bet/
beat (beat, beaten) /bi:t ('bi:tn)/
seriously ill /'sɪərɪəsli 'ɪl/

Additional material

Lesson 7A, Exercise 1

Brighton in the Rain

I've never been to Athens and I've never been to Rome
I've only seen the Pyramids in picture books at home
I've never sailed across the sea or been inside a plane
I've always spent my holidays in Brighton in the rain.

I've never eaten foreign food or drunk in a foreign bar
I've never kissed a foreign girl or driven a foreign car
I've never had to find my way in a country I don't know
I've always known just where I am and where I'll never go.

I've read travel books by writers who have been to Pakistan
I've heard people telling stories of adventures in Iran
I've watched TV documentaries about China and Brazil
But I've never been abroad myself; it's making me feel ill.

I've studied several languages like Hindi and Malay
I've learnt lots of useful sentences I've never been able to say
The furthest place I've ever been was to the Isle of Man
And that was full of tourists from Jamaica and Japan.

I've never been to Athens and I've never been to Rome
I've only seen the Pyramids in picture books at home
I've never sailed across the sea or been inside a plane
I've always spent my holidays in Brighton in the rain.

Jonathan Dykes (lyrics)
Robert Campbell (music)

Lesson 9B, Exercise 7

You Made Me Love You

You made me love you
I didn't wanna do it
I didn't wanna do it
You made me love you
And all the time you knew it
I guess you always knew it.
You made me happy, sometimes
You made me glad
But there were times when
You made me feel so sad.

You made me sigh, 'cause
I didn't wanna tell you
I didn't wanna tell you
I think you're grand, that's true,
Yes I do, 'deed I do, you know I do
Gimme, gimme, gimme, gimme
What I cry for
You know you've got the kind of kisses
That I'd die for
You know you made me love you.

(Monaco and McCarthy)

Lesson 10A, Exercise 8

Song for a Rainy Sunday

It's a rainy Sunday morning and I don't know what to do
If I stay in bed all day, I'll only think about you
If I try to study, I won't learn anything new
And if I go for a walk on my own in the park,
I'll probably catch the flu!

I just don't know (He doesn't know)
What to do (What to do)
I just don't know (He doesn't know)
What to do (What to do)

If I stay in bed all day, I'll only think about you
If I try to study, I won't learn anything new
And if I go for a walk on my own in the park,
I'll probably catch the flu – atchoo!

It's nearly Sunday lunchtime and I don't know where to eat
If I walk to the fish and chip shop, I'll only get wet feet
If I stay at home for lunch, I'll have to eat last week's meat
And if I get in my car and drive to the pub, I probably won't
   get a seat

I just don't know (He doesn't know)
Where to eat (Where to eat)
I just don't know (He doesn't know)
Where to eat (Where to eat)

If I walk to the fish and chip shop, I'll only get wet feet
If I stay at home for lunch, I'll have to eat last week's meat
And if I get in my car and drive to the pub, I probably won't
   get a seat

The rain has stopped and I'd like to go out
But I don't know where to go
If I invite you out for a drink, you'll probably say no
If I go to the theatre alone, I won't enjoy the show
And if I stay here at home on my own, I'll be bored and
   miserable, so

I just don't know (He doesn't know)
Where to go (Where to go)
I just don't know (He doesn't know)
Where to go (Where to go)

If I invite you out for a drink, you'll probably say no
If I go to the theatre alone, I won't enjoy the show
And if I stay here at home on my own, I'll be bored and
   miserable, so

I'm going to the theatre but I don't know what to wear
I know if I look through my socks I'll never find a pair
If I put on my new green boots people will probably stare
And if my tie isn't straight and they complain 'cause I'm late,
I'll say, 'Listen, mate: I don't care!'

I just don't care (He doesn't care)
What I wear (Life isn't fair)
I just don't care (He doesn't care)
What I wear (Life isn't fair)

I know if I look through my socks I'll never find a pair
If I put on my new green boots people will probably stare
And if my tie isn't straight and they complain 'cause I'm late,
I'll say, 'Listen, mate: I don't care!'

Jonathan Dykes (lyrics)
Robert Campbell (music)

Lesson 13A, Exercise 10

The Island

Each night I dream of a beautiful island
Surrounded by beaches and covered in flowers.
Butterflies dance through the sweet-smelling meadows
And birds sing their love songs for hours.

Crystal clear water runs down from the mountains
And flows through deep valleys as a sparkling stream.
Gentle sea breezes blow over my island
While sunshine pours over my dream.

Each night I visit the island of my dreams,
Each night I visit the island of my dreams,
I leave the real world behind,
It's somewhere deep in my mind,
Not too easy to find,
The island.

Bright orange squirrels play games in the tree tops
And chase through the branches where nightingales sing.
It looks so peaceful I wish I could take you
To where each night's the first day of spring.

Chorus.

I leave the real world behind,
It's somewhere deep in my mind,
Not too easy to find,
The island.

The island.   The island.

Jonathan Dykes (lyrics)
Robert Campbell (music)

Lesson 14B, Dialogue B

MOTHER: Can I speak to you for a minute, Em?
DAUGHTER: ....
MOTHER: Well, I'm very upset about how late you were
           out last night.
DAUGHTER: ....
MOTHER: I still think that's too late for a fifteen-year-old
           girl who has to go to school the next day.
DAUGHTER: ....
MOTHER: Well, you're not all the other kids. And I'm sure
           some of them have to be in early.
DAUGHTER: ....
MOTHER: Especially on school nights. I don't want you in
           after ten when you've got school the next day.
DAUGHTER: ....
MOTHER: Well, if there's a special night we can talk about
           it before you go. I'm sure we can agree if we
           talk about it.
DAUGHTER: ....
MOTHER: Thanks, darling.

Unit 19 Dialogues

DIALOGUE 1

(The doorbell rings.)

PETER: I'll go.
ANN: OK.

(Peter opens the door.)

PETER: Hello, hello. Nice to see you.
SUE: Hello, Peter. Are we late!
PETER: No, not at all. You're the first, actually.
JOHN: Oh, good. Who else is coming?
PETER: Come in and have a drink. Well, there's Don and
        Emma, Jo and Stephen, and my sister Lucy and her
        new boyfriend. Can't remember his name. Let me
        take your coat. You know Lucy, don't you?
SUE: I think we've met her once.
ANN: Hello, Sue. Hello, John. Lovely to see you. I'm so
        glad you could come. Now, what can I get you to
        drink?

SUE: What have you got?
ANN: Oh, the usual things. Sherry; gin and tonic – I think;
        vodka; I think there's some beer; a glass of
        wine . . . ?
SUE: I'll have a gin and tonic, Ann, please.
JOHN: So will I.
SUE: Doesn't the room look nice, John? You've changed it
        round since we were here last, haven't you? The
        piano was, let me see, yes, the piano was over by
        the window, wasn't it?
PETER: That's right. And we've moved the sofa over there
        and . . .

DIALOGUE 2

JOHN: So you work in a pub.
LUCY: Yes, that's right.
JOHN: What's it like?
LUCY: It's nice. I like it. You meet a lot of interesting
        people. A lot of boring ones too, mind you.
JOHN: I beg your pardon?
LUCY: I said, a lot of boring ones too.
JOHN: Oh, yes. I can imagine. A pub – I should think that's
        hard work, isn't it?
LUCY: Yes and no. It depends.
JOHN: How do you mean?
LUCY: Well, it's hard at weekends. I mean, last Saturday
        night, with both bars full and one barman away ill –
        well, my feet didn't touch the ground. But on
        weekdays it's usually very quiet.
        What about you? What do you do? You're an
        accountant or something, aren't you?
JOHN: I work in a bank.
LUCY: Oh yes, that's right. Ann said. That must be nice.
JOHN: It's all right.
LUCY: But you have to move round from one place to
        another, don't you? I mean, if you get a better job – if
        they make you manager or something – it'll probably
        be in another town, won't it?
JOHN: Yes, probably.
LUCY: I wouldn't like that. I mean, I've got lots of friends
        here. I wouldn't like to move somewhere else.
JOHN: Oh, we like it. We've lived here for, what, six years
        now. We're ready for a change.

DIALOGUE 3

DON: Have you got the salt down your end, Steve?
STEPHEN: What are you looking for?
DON: The salt.
STEPHEN: Salt. Salt. Oh, yes. Here it is. And could you pass
         me the mustard in exchange?
         This is delicious beef, Ann. Who's your butcher?
ANN: Not telling you.
         What are John and Lucy talking about?
JOHN: Work, I'm afraid.
SUE: I thought so. It's all John ever talks about. Work
         and food.
JOHN: Well, there are worse things in life. Especially if
         the food's like this.
ANN: Thank you, John. Would you like some more?
         Have another potato. Some more meat. Some
         beans. A carrot. A piece of bread.
JOHN: No, thanks. That was lovely, but I've had enough.
         Really. I'll have another glass of wine, perhaps.
EMMA: Here you are, John.

         (Crash!)

         Oh, damn! I *am* sorry, Ann. How stupid of me.
ANN: That's all right. It doesn't matter at all. Really.
         They're very cheap glasses.

DIALOGUE 4

ANDY: I didn't like it at all.

EMMA: Oh, I thought it was lovely.

JOHN: It was rubbish. Complete rubbish. Absolute nonsense.

ANN: I didn't think much of it, I must say.

LUCY: I liked it. At the end, when she was dying, I cried. I couldn't help it. I cried and cried.

STEPHEN: Jo said it made her laugh.

JO: No, I didn't. Oh, Steve, you are awful! Really! No, it's just that – I don't know – it didn't say anything to me.

JOHN: I'm afraid I must be very old-fashioned, but I like things to have a beginning, a middle and an end.

STEPHEN: Yes, so do I.

JOHN: And I *don't* like a lot of sex and violence.

EMMA: Oh, I love sex and violence!

ANN: More coffee, anybody?

ANDY: I don't like violence.

EMMA: But listen. Why didn't you like it? I thought it was great. Really.

ANN: So wordy. It was really really boring. They just talked and talked and talked all the time.

STEPHEN: I can't stand –

EMMA: No, look –

LUCY: I don't think –

DON: Three old women sitting around talking for two and a half hours. If that's what you want, you might as well go and spend the evening in the old people's home.

LUCY: It wasn't like that at all.

ANDY: Yes it was.

LUCY: No it wasn't.

ANDY: Yes it was.

ANN :   Who wrote it, anyway?

JO: Don't know. What's his name? Fred Walker, something like that.

ANDY: Who's he?

DON: Never heard of him.

STEPHEN: Didn't he write . . .

DIALOGUE 5

DON: Well, I'm afraid it's getting late, and we've got a long way to go.

SUE: So have we. We ought to be on our way, I suppose.

JO: Yes, we'd better be going, too. Thank you so much, Ann. We really enjoyed ourselves. Lovely food, nice people, good talk, . . .

ANN: Well, thank you for coming.

EMMA: You must come over to us soon. When we've finished moving. I'll give you a ring.

JOHN: Now, where's my coat?

PETER: Here it is, John.

JOHN: No, that's not mine. This is mine.

PETER: Oh, sorry. Well, whose is this, then?

ANN: Andy's, I think.

ANDY: Is it old and dirty? Yes, that's mine.

LUCY: Well, bye, Ann, bye, Peter. See you next week.

EVERYBODY: Bye, bye.

Lesson 14B, Dialogue A

MOTHER: . . . .

DAUGHTER: Sure, Mum, what's the problem?

MOTHER: . . . .

DAUGHTER: But Mum, I was in by twelve o'clock!

MOTHER: . . . .

DAUGHTER: Well, I don't think so. All the other kids stay out late.

MOTHER: . . . .

DAUGHTER: Yeah, some of them do, I suppose.

MOTHER: . . . .

DAUGHTER: But last night was special. It was the disco at the club.

MOTHER: . . . .

DAUGHTER: All right, Mum. Perhaps you're right. I'll talk to you about it next time.

MOTHER: . . . .

Lesson 23B, Exercise 8

Trying to Love Two Women

Trying to love two women
Is like a ball and chain
Trying to love two women
Is like a ball and chain
Sometimes the pleasure
Ain't worth the strain
It's a long old grind
And it tires your mind

Trying to hold two women
Is tearing me apart
Trying to hold two women
Is tearing me apart
One's got my money
And the other's got my heart
It's a long old grind
And it tires your mind

When you try to please two women
You can't please yourself
When you try to please two women
You can't please yourself
Your best is only half good
A man can't stock two shelves
It's a long old grind,
And it tires your mind

(first verse twice)   *(Sonny Throckmorton)*

Lesson 25B, Exercise 2

The Riddle Song

I gave my love a cherry, it had no stone
I gave my love a chicken without a bone
I told my love a story, it had no end
I gave my love a baby with no crying.

How can there be a cherry without a stone?
How can there be a chicken without a bone?
How can there be a story that has no end?
How can there be a baby with no crying?

Well a cherry when it's blooming, it has no stone
A chicken when it's pipping, it has no bone
The story of I love you, it has no end
A baby when it's sleeping has no crying.

The Riddle Song by Harry Robinson and Julie Felix, © 1965, TRO Essex Music Ltd.

Logger Lover

As I walked out one evening
'Twas in a small cafe
A forty-year-old waitress
To me these words did say:

I see that you are a logger
And not just a common bum
For nobody but a logger
Stirs his coffee with his thumb.

My lover, he was a logger
There's none like him today
If you poured whisky upon it
He would eat a bale of hay.

My lover came to see me
'Twas on one winter's day
He held me in his fond embrace
And broke three vertebrae.

He kissed me when he left me
So hard he broke my jaw
And I could not speak to tell him
He'd forgot his mackinaw.

Well, the weather tried to freeze him
It did its level best
At one hundred degrees below zero
Well, he buttoned up his vest.

It froze clear through to China,
It froze to the stars above
At one thousand degrees below zero
It froze my logger love.

And so I lost my lover
To this cafe I did come
And here I wait till someone
Stirs his coffee with his thumb.

(Traditional)

What Did You Learn in School Today?

What did you learn in school today,
Dear little boy of mine?
What did you learn in school today,
Dear little boy of mine?
I learned that Washington never told a lie,
I learned that soldiers seldom die,
I learned that everybody's free,
That's what the teacher said to me,
And that's what I learned in school today,
That's what I learned in school.

What did you learn in school today,
Dear little boy of mine?
What did you learn in school today,
Dear little boy of mine?
I learned that policemen are my friends,
I learned that justice never ends,
I learned that murderers die for their crimes,
Even if we make a mistake sometimes,
And that's what I learned in school today,
That's what I learned in school.

What did you learn in school today,
Dear little boy of mine?
What did you learn in school today,
Dear little boy of mine?

I learned our government must be strong,
It's always right and never wrong,
Our leaders are the finest men,
And we elect them again and again,
And that's what I learned in school today,
That's what I learned in school.

(Tom Paxton)

Memory Test for Lesson 29A, Exercise 6

Acknowledgements

The authors and publishers are grateful to the following copyright owners for permission to reproduce photographs, illustrations, texts and music. Every endeavour has been made to contact copyright owners and apologies are expressed for any omissions.

page 21: Reproduced by permission of Syndication International.   page 31: Reproduced by permission of *Punch*.   page 39: Reproduced by permission of British Telecom.   page 60: *cl* 'My mother said . . .' from *God Bless Love*, Nanette Newman (Collins, 1972), © Invalid Children's Association, reproduced by kind permission of ICA. *tc, br* 'Dear God . . .', 'If they don't want . . .' from *Children's Letters to God* (Fontana, Collins, 1976), reproduced by permission of the Publisher. *cr* 'My mum only likes . . .' from Extracts from Nanette Newman's Collections of Sayings, by permission of the authors, © reserved.   page 61: From Extracts from Nanette Newman's Collection of Sayings, by permission of the authors, © reserved.   page 92: *tr* Courtesy of John, Hairdresser, Croydon, *cr* Mobil Oil Company Limited.   page 93: *tr* Courtesy of Joan Galleli, The Shirley Poppy.   page 96: *b* Reproduced by permission of *Punch*.   page 98: From the *Longman Active Study Dictionary of English* edited by Della Summers, Longman 1983.   page 102: *tr* Photographie Musée National d'Art Moderne, Centre Georges Pompidou, Paris. *tl* Reproduced by courtesy of the Trustees, The National Gallery, London. *bl* Reproduced by courtesy of the Board of Trustees of the Victoria and Albert Museum.   page 104: *l* Courtesy of Gallery Lingard. *r* Reproduced from the poster of the London Mozart Players 1984–1985. *c* Reproduced from London Features International Ltd.   page 113: From an article by Anna Tomforde in the *Guardian* – adapted. page 115: Reproduced by permission of *Punch*.   page 116: *t* Reproduced by permission of *Punch*. *b* From *Weekend Book of Jokes* 21 (Harmsworth Publications Ltd.), reproduced by permission of Associated Newspapers Plc.   page 117: Reproduced by permission of Syndication International. page 124: 'My dad . . .', 'A prime minister . . .' 'When you grow up . . .' Reproduced by permission of Bryan Forbes Ltd.   page 128: Nos. 1-7, 10 from *The Highway Code* (Her Majesty's Stationery Office), Reproduced by permission of the Publisher. Colour details: 1. green light showing. Other lights are red (top) and amber (middle). 2. same as (1) except that red light is showing. 3. red triangle, white background, black letters. 4. white circle, red background, white horizontal line. 5. red circle and diagonal, white background, black directional sign. 6. red circle, white background, black man. 7. red triangle, white background, black car and lines. 8. grey road, yellow double lines, white dotted lines. 9. grey road, white lines. 10. red triangle, white background, black rocks.   page 131: *tl* McLachlan. *tr, c, bl* Reproduced by permission of *Punch*. *br* Reproduced by permission of Syndication International.   page 156: Song *You Made Me Love You*, lyrics: Joe McCarthy, music: James V. Monaco © 1913 Broadway Music Corp, USA. Sub-published by Francis Day & Hunter Ltd., London WC2H 0LD. Reproduced by permission of EMI Music Publishing Ltd. and International Music Publications.   page 158: Song *Trying to Love Two Women*, by Sonny Throckmorton, © Cross Keys Publishing Company Inc., USA. Sub-published by EMI Music Publishing Ltd., London WC2H 0LD. Reproduced by permission of EMI Publishing Ltd. and International Music Publications.   page 158: Song *The Riddle Song* by Harry Robinson & Julie Felix, © 1965 TRO Essex Music Ltd., Bury Place, London WC1A 2LA for the World International Copyright secured. All Rights Reserved.   page 159: The version of the song *Logger Lover*

is by Dick Stephenson and is used with permission.   page 159: *What Did You Learn in School Today?*, words and music by Tom Paxton. Reprinted by permission of Harmony Music Limited, 19/20 Poland Street, London W1V 3DD.

The songs *Brighton in the Rain* (Lesson 7A, page 156), *Song for a Rainy Sunday* (Lesson 10A, page 156), *The Island* (Lesson 13A, page 156), *My Old Dad* (Lesson 14A, page 59), *Another Street Incident* (Lesson 17B, page 72), and *A Bigger Heart* (Lesson 22A, page 90) were specially written for *The Cambridge English Course* Book 2 by Jonathan Dykes (lyrics) and Robert Campbell (music). The recorded material for Lesson 11A, Exercise 4 (page 181) and Revision Tests 1 (page 166) and 2 (page 170) is used by kind permission of Wiltshire Radio.

Ace Photo Agency: p92 *l*.   BBC Hulton Picture Library: p110 *br*.   Camera Press Limited: p110 *tr*, nos. 2, 3, *c* (Margaret Thatcher), *b* (second from *l*).   The Daily Telegraph: pages 98 *l*, 122 (teacher, farmer, 3 industrial photos). p50: *tc* Courtesy of Jaakko Poyry (UK) Limited. London Features International Limited: p104 *c*. Monitor Picture Library: p93 *tl, br*.   Pictorial Press Limited: p110 *b* (second from *r*).   Alan Philip: pages 6–7, 36, 64.   The Press Association: p95 *t*.   Doc Rowe: p105.   Spectrum Colour Library: pages 36–37, 98 *r*. Sporting Pictures UK Limited: p95 *b*.   Syndication International Limited: pages 110 *tc, cr*, nos. 1, 4, *bl*, 122 (housewife, nurse).   John Topham Picture Library: pages 68, 74–75. p125: © United Kingdom Atomic Energy Authority, used with permission.   Reg van Cuÿlenburg: pages 22, 63, 66–67.   Catherine Walter: p8.   Wiggins Teape Group: p50 *tr, br*.   Jason Youé: pages 92 *tr, cr*, 93 *tr, cl, cr*, 125 *t*.

John Craddock: Malcolm Barter, pages 14 *t*, 37 *b*, 38–39, 58, 69 *b*, 78–79, 80–81;   Alexa Rutherford, pages 20, 28, 59, 94, 108 *t*, 120;   Kate Simunek, p57;   Ian Fleming and Associates Limited: Terry Burton, p100;   David Lewis Management: Odette Buchanan, pages 18, 45, 91, 112;   Bob Harvey, pages 40, 41 *r*, 65, 69 *t*, 72, 88, 113, 121 *t*;   Jon Miller, pages 10–11, 84, 121 *b*;   Linda Rogers: Mike Whittlesea, pages 27, 44 *b*, 71 *l*, 82 *t*, 108 *b*, 114 *t*;   Linden Artists Limited: Jon Davis, pages 30 *b*, 35, 70, 126–127;   Val Sangster, pages 16, 24, 71 *r*, 96 *t*, 114 *b*.

Paul Davenport, pages 44 *t*, 52–53, 76;   Paul Francis, pages 14 *b*, 15;   Martin Gordon, p42;   Gary Inwood, pages 41 *l*, 43, 73, 82 *b*, 123;   Jane Molineaux, pages 26, 77;   Chris Rawlings, pages 30 *t*, 33;   Nik Spender, pages 12–13, 56, 83, 118, 132–133;   Tony Streek, pages 23, 34, 54 *t*, 89, 119;   Malcolm Ward, pages 19, 54 *b*, 86, 109, 111, Jack Wood, pages 51, 54 *b*, 55, 112;   Mike Woodhatch, pages 106–107;   John Youe & Associates.

(Abbreviations: *t*=top   *b*=bottom   *c*=centre   *r*=right *l*=left)